D0194894

Expand your
world without leaving
your hometown

The Art of Being a Tourist at Home

Jenny Herbert

Hardie Grant

T R A V E L

Contents

Part two: Worlds within worlds

Part three: The pleasures of being grounded

Afterword

In memory of my dear Mum
1926–2020

*'Though we often take long journeys, and cross the seas
to examine curiosities, we neglect them when they lie
beneath our very eye.'*

Pliny the Younger (61–113 CE)

Writing in a time of pandemic

I started writing this book in 2019 when it seemed possible to speculate, with a fair degree of confidence, on where we were heading. Travel was contributing eight per cent of global emissions and overtourism was destroying ecosystems and communities. The climate crisis was the planet's number one threat.

Change came rapidly and dramatically in early 2020. The impact of COVID-19 is so unprecedented that forecasting in its wake has become impossible. Lacking a crystal ball, I have tried to map a path through self-isolation, social distancing, travel restrictions and closed borders with a gradual return to some form of normality. But books, once printed, become sealed in their moment in time while life moves on, so there's every chance that some of what I have written is already out-of-date or has not yet returned to our lives.

Yet despite some possible flawed assumptions, my overall message remains relevant and true. There exists all around us, *at home*, so much to add value to our lives and to fortify us against disruption and disorder.

The pandemic has not lessened our obligations to future generations. The climate crisis remains our biggest global challenge. An altered approach to the ways in which we travel is still needed.

Introduction

The story begins at home

'It is not down on any map; true places never are.'

Herman Melville

Holiday virtues

Holidays are good for us. They help us to recalibrate and renew. They have the power to reduce stress, revitalise relationships and improve our mental and physical health. They disrupt our normal routines, stimulate curiosity and introduce new ways of seeing.

Achieving all of this and more shouldn't be based on how much money we spend or how far we go. But when the first jumbo jets soared into the skies in the 1970s they took our holiday expectations with them. In a remarkably short time international travel skyrocketed. Our first thought when planning a holiday became, where will we fly to? Real holidays came to mean stamps in passports; fun and adventure were only to be found at the end of a long flight.

Do we really need to go far to have rewarding holidays? Through the following chapters I want to explore honestly what we want our holidays to achieve – stripped of all of the travel hype – and how the experiences that truly enrich our lives in meaningful and enduring ways are just as readily found at home.

Staycations

The word staycation – meaning stay-at-home vacation – entered our vocabulary in 2005. Even back then it wasn't about being confined within four walls with little to do. As the world has come to face multiple crises that reduce our desire or ability to travel, staycations have grown in popularity, scope and appeal. Their goal is to celebrate the spirit of travel without the need for going great distances.

What we call home can be as local as our street and neighbourhood or as expansive as our city, region or country. The emphasis is on reigning in our impact on the planet, not denying ourselves enjoyable holidays. Staycation benefits include reducing stress, saving money, making good use of every moment of our leisure time and supporting our local businesses and community.

How we spend our at home time can be as varied, creative, relaxing or energising as any overseas travel. We set the pace. We can be as flexible as we wish with our plans. And everything we learn, every old habit discarded, every new interest pursued, can be woven into our everyday life, even when we return to our everyday world.

Best of all, staycations give us the space and time to meditate on what really matters and what truly gives meaning to our life. We are our most genuine selves at home, which makes it the best place to explore what imbues our existence with purpose.

Travel promotions use the lure of happiness to draw us away. While happiness is a wonderfully uplifting mood, it is as transient as any trip. Our quest for meaning in life is a lifelong journey, with contentment as its more enduring goal. At home in ourselves, at one with the world, we can be grateful for what we have.

While searching for meaning in life can be our most rewarding journey, it can seem like a daunting task and there's so much else demanding our attention. It's as if we're afraid of the quest and what it might reveal and demand of us. Instead, we pore over travel websites and dream of exotic destinations as if they offer all the answers. Stoked by the *discontentment* those websites arouse, we book a flight, pack our bags and fly away.

Not asking too much

Many years ago, the British cookery writer Elizabeth David published a collection of her newspaper columns under the title *An Omelette and a Glass of Wine*. It's a wonderful title, speaking of home, contentment and a celebration of life's simple pleasures.

There's nothing fancy about an omelette, yet this modest dish, accompanied by a glass of wine, provides all we ask of a meal: visual appeal, flavour and nourishment. I can picture the table set with a candle and flowers, the ruby glow of pinot noir and two fluffy golden omelettes folded around a handful of freshly picked herbs.

Such simple perfection gives us a feeling of quiet satisfaction, reminding us that the best of life is not dependent on grand flourishes or expensive adornment.

This planet, our home

Staycations make such good sense. They're closer, cheaper, easier. They're less stressful. They're better for our health and the planet.

This Earth is our place of residence, but we are Gaia's lodgers, not landlords. As travellers, we have largely ignored our obligations as guests. We have taken a privilege as our right and, in vast swarms, we've trampled over every corner of Mother Earth's realm, to reach this point where her five-star accommodation is being reduced to a slum.

'This is not a drill,' the Swedish environmental activist Greta Thunberg reminds us. Aware that individuals must act now to save the planet, her personal protest led to a global environmental movement. In 2019, addressing the UN Climate Summit, she said, 'This is all wrong. I shouldn't be up here ... yet you all come to us young people for hope. How dare you!' Delegates gave her a standing ovation.

In that same year, a photograph appeared in newspapers around the world that came to symbolised overtourism: hundreds of climbers queueing for their turn on the Mount Everest summit. That photo and Greta Thunberg's determination have, surely, robbed us of our complacency.

Along with the climate crisis and overtourism, the COVID-19 pandemic has also caused us to reconsider our decisions about travel. There are other trends – amplified by our experiences of self-isolation – causing us to reassess how we live. A growing desire to consume less, to lead simpler, less cluttered lives, to prioritise wellbeing. There's a growing enlightenment, too, that the trappings of wealth (including the opportunity to travel) do not automatically bestow happiness and certainly not contentment.

By choice or by necessity, we are coming to appreciate that there's more to our immediate surroundings than we had credited. All the travel tropes – self-discovery, tolerance, better health, wider knowledge and improved social skills – are achievable at home. This is where we truly come to know who we are and our place in the world.

I'm certainly not advocating that all future travel plans should be abandoned. Travel will always have its place: to pursue a special interest; family calls us home; there's one last item on our bucket list. What I am proposing is that we consider travel as just one option. An alternative course is to turn our attention to the amazing kaleidoscope of possibilities if we vacation at home.

When the architect Max Dupain was asked why he didn't like to travel abroad, he answered with these lines from William Blake's poem *Auguries of Innocence*, 'To see a world in a grain of sand/And a heaven in a wild flower ...'

By choice or by necessity, we are coming to appreciate that there's more to our immediate surroundings than we had credited. All the travel tropes – self-discovery, tolerance, better health, wider knowledge and improved social skills – are achievable at home. This is where we truly come to know who we are and our place in the world.

Come travel with me

In the following pages, we will explore our neighbourhood, visit farmers' markets and streets full of foreign languages and foods. We'll check out museums, libraries, and theatres. Along the way, we'll tune in to music and puzzle over art. We'll take in some cooking, learning, sport and hobbies. We'll make time for daydreaming, playing and reading. We'll examine our notions of home and how we need to break old routines and habits to see things anew.

So come travel with me through these pages and I'll show you that the world on your doorstep is as wonderful, exciting, surprising and inspiring as any foreign land.

Part one

Go your own way

Why do we travel?

'Independence ... is loyalty to one's best self and principles'.

Mark Twain

A changed world

Why do we travel? Is it to see iconic places, to visit friends and family, to break the routine, to learn, to have fun, to be pampered, to shop? Yes, certainly, it can be for all these reasons. It might be to tick off an item on your bucket list, to collect anecdotes for dinner parties, or to take the perfect Instagram shot. Or maybe it's because we have all the possessions we need and are looking for another way to spend our money. Or that the grass always seems greener somewhere else.

Is it because we are easily swayed by the marketers who tell us that we are lesser beings without a passport full of stamps? We want to believe that we are capable of making up our own mind rationally, but the reality is our decisions are mostly emotion-based and groupthink often has the stronger say.

Maybe it is that we give little thought to our reasons for travel. We simply pack our bags and go.

Or at least we did, until our jet-setting ways came to an abrupt halt in 2020 and we looked, amazed, at photographs of blue skies over Beijing and fish in Venetian canals. Despite the economic disaster of lost tourism income, the tortoises of the Galapagos Islands must have breathed a sigh of relief. Streets stripped bare of visiting hordes opened the way for new relationships between residents and their cities.

These positive changes gave us real pause for thought and inescapable evidence of the negative impacts of travel. They turned our minds towards the opportunities and virtues of staying home.

Weigh up both sides

Until recently, travel wasn't for everyone. There were pilgrimages, merchant voyages and Grand Tours, but most people lived their entire lives within the boundaries of their village, town or city. They might have ventured to the next town within walking distance, for matters of trade, but holidays were holy days and their observance was centred on home, church and the market square.

Perhaps it's our era's wealth and access to cheap and easy transportation more than inherent wanderlust that sends us on our journeys.

While the internet is awash with all the positives about why we should travel, there have always been dissenting voices. Ralph Waldo Emerson said it brought 'ruins to the ruins'. And Marcel Proust wrote that, 'the real voyage of discovery consists not in seeking new landscapes, but in having new eyes'.

Like many others, Paul Theroux was at pains to apply a measure of status by distinguishing travellers from tourists (travellers being trail-blazing adventurers, tourists mere followers). While the American journalist Elizabeth Drew noted that travel was more likely to lengthen conversations than broaden minds.

The debate has washed back and forth. The phenomenal growth in tourist numbers has made us ambivalent towards travel, as we've become more aware of the damage our travels have unwittingly inflicted on host communities, natural environments and, indeed, the planet.

How should we live?

Has our pursuit of the good life, with its attendant wealth and consumption, made us blind to what is most important? Have we forgotten to ask ourselves how we should live in a way that is most likely to achieve meaning in life?

In searching for an answer we might examine the way in which travel can crowd out what really matters: home, belonging, relationships. We might

The phenomenal growth in tourist numbers has made us ambivalent towards travel, as we've become more aware of the damage our travels have unwittingly inflicted on host communities, natural environments and, indeed, the planet.

also ask, in terms of contemporary concerns and obligations: How should we live in these times of uncertainty and rapid change? How should we live in ways that minimise damage?

We might more honestly examine travel's downsides. It can be lonely, uncomfortable, fatiguing, tedious and disappointing. It can, on occasion, be frightening. And what of the financial strain? Most people identify financial concerns as the major cause of their stress and acknowledge that the best coping mechanism is adjusting expectations.

It is within ourselves – not out in the world – where we must find our answers. Independent-mindedness is the key to deciding what is best for *us* and resisting the social and commercial forces that try to control our choices. In place of consumption we can choose contentment, acceptance, gratitude, with who we are, what we have, and how we live.

Finding home

In the 1920s American writer Henry Beston spent a year living alone on an isolated stretch of the Maine coastline. In the book that he wrote of his experience – *The Outermost House: a Year of Life on the Great Beach of Cape Cod* – we follow him through the seasons and through his ever-growing affinity with his remote home as he observed and recorded the world constantly changing around him.

He wrote of storms more fantastic than fireworks displays and of the surf's world of sounds. In this one place – his home – he showed what is gained when we engage our five senses, how the tiniest details open up new vistas of understanding. Everything weaves together into a whole that becomes a sense of place. The deep and satisfying attachment that can only be achieved by taking the time and making the effort to be acutely attuned to one's surroundings.

As this was the 1920s Beston wasn't observing his world through a smartphone, nor did he allow his vision to be constrained by the lens of a camera. He committed to memory what he saw through his naked eye, then put what he had observed into words. Reading those words a hundred years later we relearn what we have forgotten. We discover ourselves through our sensual experience of what is immediately around us. This is how we connect to a place and come to know who we are.

We are shaped by where we live. The external becomes internal. This is what John Steinbeck discovered when he drove across the United States with his dog Charley in an attempt to find what it meant to be American. In his book *Travels with Charley*, he explained how America revealed itself to be a larger version of himself. And only he, as an American, would see his homeland in this way. People from other countries could make the same journey, but their interpretations of what they saw and heard would be completely different.

> ## We are shaped by where we live. The external becomes internal.

Where to begin?

We'll start our exploration of home by putting into practice, locally, the sort of activities we undertake when far away. Walking unfamiliar streets, paying attention to detail, visiting parks and gardens, and meeting people of different nationalities. We'll discover how all of these activities can be easily pursued close to home, with the same or greater rewards. We'll challenge the myth that we should and must travel.

Free to roam

'Two or three hours' walking will carry me to as strange a country as I expect ever to see.'

Henry David Thoreau

Look again

Years ago, on a Sunday morning in Rome, I rose before dawn and went for a walk in what might have been a completely different city. No traffic, no noise other than church bells ringing and pigeons cooing. I passed only a few people: drowsy carabinieri in the Piazza del Popolo; couples with linked arms on their way to early Mass; waiters setting up outdoor tables. They each offered a quiet buon giorno. The city belonged to them alone.

The Trevi Fountain and Spanish Steps were deserted; the churches were the preserve of a few parishioners. I strolled wherever my steps took me and watched the grand metropolis come slowly to life as cafés opened, traffic built, and the Via del Corso filled with shoppers. It was a rare experience and all it took was a walk at an uncommon time of day.

Many years later I repeated this dawn walk at home. That I should meet the unfamiliar in a foreign city was understandable, experiencing *my* city as a place unknown was disorienting. I found novelty everywhere I looked and so discovered that a place doesn't have to be foreign to be eye-opening.

When COVID-19 rendered our cities and towns empty and silent by decree, newspapers filled with photographs of deserted streets, abandoned railway stations and airports, empty shopping malls. For the first time in living memory public spaces were stripped bare of bustling crowds. There was a hint of the romance we see in ruins, a sense of estrangement.

It was, like my dawn ramble through Rome, a unique chance to see familiar places utterly changed.

Rhythm of life

Walking makes us healthier, happier and smarter. The rhythm promotes thinking, creativity, contemplation, story-making. Walking with others bestows a joyous synchronicity. It's not *just* exercise, it's not *just* about reaching a destination. It's about being at one with our physical environment. It's a brilliant way of cementing our sense of place.

Walking gives us uninterrupted time to think through our worries and map out solutions. Its rhythm unwinds us and lets in contentment. In a positive state of mind, we become more alert to the details and loveliness of our surroundings. We smile at the surprises.

The French use the word flâneur, meaning someone who strolls. Wandering wherever their curiosity leads them, resistant to haste or pressure, free to get lost. Although there's a suggestion of aimlessness, the true flâneur's amble is nonchalant but rarely purposeless. It's not about reaching a destination, it's about being alert to whatever presents itself along the way.

To flâneur at home is to discover rich possibilities in our immediate world. There's surprise with every turn simply because we *thought* we knew the landscape. To actually go hunting for the previously unseen, we find ourselves asking over and over, 'how is it that I have never noticed this before?'

In her book *Wanderlust*, Rebecca Solnit wrote of how the mind, body and world align when we walk. Henry David Thoreau loved the word sauntering. He believed that it 'is itself the enterprise and the adventure of the day [that lets] more air and sunshine into our thoughts'. (It goes without saying that if the flâneur owns a mobile phone it will be turned off and tucked away in a pocket or handbag for the duration of the walk.)

There are local shops to inspect, the park to stroll through, gardens to be admired. There's street art to ponder and different quarters to explore.

Stroll with curiosity

The author and activist Jane Jacobs first used the term walkability to describe walking as a way of promoting curiosity and connection. As we walk and look, Jacobs suggested, we should also listen, linger, and think about what we are seeing. She loved the idea of what she called the sidewalk ballet of people interacting with each other.

There are local shops to inspect, the park to stroll through, gardens to be admired. There's street art to ponder and different quarters to explore. There are surreptitious peeks to be had through gaps in fences and rarely opened gates. There are chance eye contacts and exchanged smiles with strangers. There's the possibility of turning a corner and finding ourselves caught up in a tableau of human joy or drama.

We might look at the familiar from unconventional angles. Thoreau once climbed a tall pine tree and saw mountains he didn't know existed. 'I might have walked about the foot of the tree for threescore years and ten, and yet I certainly should never have seen them.'

Home's history

How strange that we go to the trouble of researching the places we visit but rarely put the same effort into finding out about the place where we live.

While walking the local streets, we might ask: When was this suburb first settled and why? How was this street named? Why are most of the houses built in stone? Are these street's trees endemic to this region?

This new thirst for knowledge – to know what has shaped our home – is easily slaked. All we need to do is extend our walk as far as the local library. There we'll discover books that have been written specifically about our place.

The Australian writer Barry Dickens published a novel set in the suburb where both he and I grew up. Reading his reminiscences gave me the odd feeling of reliving my childhood through his keener vision. With my brothers, I laughed and cried at the truths Dickens mocked, revered and celebrated.

Walk back in time

We can walk across town and we can walk back in time. Returning to old haunts rekindles forgotten memories through sights, sounds and smells – the biographical landmarks of our younger selves.

The writer Alfred Kazin took such a journey back in time, returning as an adult to walk the streets of his childhood. He'd grown up in Brownsville on the outskirts of New York, in a poor community of Jewish immigrants and African Americans. Kazin's purpose was to take the measure of the distance he had travelled in his life and to examine the experiences that influenced who he had become.

His walking pace allowed him to gather old memories and new impressions. His old block had become lined with second-hand furniture stores selling the items that had furnished the homes of his youth. He passed a shop that had once sold candy and tasted 'the old sweetness of malted milks'.

The grand narratives and histories are easy to find. The statues of famous forebears and monuments celebrating events of national consequence are given pride of place so that they can't be missed. They may be appealing to tourists but are not always a true rendering of history, certainly not inclusive. They may, in fact, be divisive, as demonstrated by the pulling down of statues that commemorated Confederate leaders and slave traders in the United States and elsewhere.

Rather, it's the stories of ordinary lives, recorded in day-to-day acts and glimpses, that tell a truer, more inclusive narrative. It's in the seemingly insignificant details of home that we find stories that we can relate to and be part of.

Take a different route

These days if we do walk – to work, to the bakery – we follow an undeviating route chosen for efficiency; the destination is all that matters. What if walking involved straying off the beaten track? Thrown from our routine, we're forced to be alert to what is around us. We can pretend to be strangers in town, observing without preconceptions or dismissiveness. Unlike being pulled along in the wake of a tour guide, we can stop at any time. There's no-one to tell us where to look or what to think.

Our hometown walks can be random, fragmented and therefore endlessly absorbing. We can choose to get lost. Local explorations are so much more relaxed because if we don't see everything this time, or later can't quite remember a detail, or want to know more, it's an easy matter to return. With repeated walks, we can measure the passage of time, marking the changes wrought by seasons and progress and aging and know that we are a part of these changes, in this place that is home.

Our hometown
walks can be random,
fragmented and therefore
endlessly absorbing.

Awaken our senses

I think my two Border Collies are clever when they sit, heel and fetch.
But their true talent lies in their sensory interpretation of their world.
I can take them on the same walk every afternoon and each time it will
be fresh and exciting for them, full of new smells, sights and sounds.
Watching their enthusiasm for discovery and their intense reading
of the environment is enough to lift my heart.

They're also teaching me an important lesson. We can follow the
same path every day and, if we are perceptive to the changes,
if we put our senses on high alert, it's never the same walk twice.

Seek simple wonders

On my daily walk along the beach and through the Australian bush of native
banksia and eucalypts, I find all manner of gifts from nature: silk-smooth
driftwood; gum leaves in the muted colours of old frescoes; feathers from
sea eagles, swans, rosellas. I found a bird's nest – a tightly woven basket lined
with bright red feathers – and gave it to an artist friend for her birthday.
I could have been giving her rubies.

The world on our doorstep

'We all live with the objective of being happy; our lives are all different and yet the same.'

Anne Frank

Open your mind

We love the cosmopolitan sensibility that comes with being well travelled, open-minded and at ease no matter where we are in the world. We love the sense of transformation that travel bestows, emphasised by our passports and the borders we cross. We go to witness novelty, things that aren't like home and people who aren't like us. We eat the food and exclaim over exotic tastes; we watch the locals, curious about their ways.

Mark Twain famously said that 'travel is fatal to prejudice, bigotry and narrow-mindedness'.

While that is undoubtedly true of travel's influence on many people, sadly we've all also witnessed the rude, condescending tourist who thinks that their nationality makes them superior to their hosts. Or those who smugly boast of how they bartered down the price of a meal in an impoverished community.

Yet even at our most open-minded, we remain outsiders. We never fully comprehend the nuances of age-old customs or the subtly different interpretations of the modern world. At home, we can mix far more easily, genuinely and comfortably with people of different backgrounds who are also our fellow citizens. Being in their company, learning their history and adopting some of their ways, we come to experience the glow of worldliness.

Without needing to travel, we can cultivate a cosmopolitan state of mind by exploring other cultures through music and dance, theatre and books. Our own museums tell fascinating stories that celebrate humanity in all of its splendid medley. Our art museums and galleries exhibit the art of the world. In all of these ways we learn about other perceptions and have not only our assumptions challenged but our worldview expanded and enhanced.

Simple acts can bring other cultures into our lives. It might be using a tagine to cook Moroccan chicken or playing bocce in the back yard. It can be growing previously unheard-of vegetables or learning to play a new instrument. When we deliberately go hunting, we find that there's an abundance of new ideas and interests to reveal the wonder within difference. Our discoveries invest joy and broadmindedness into our everyday. They become valuable contributions to our quest for meaning in life.

A world of difference

Historically, communities isolated by geography and without the means of transport and communication developed their individual languages and dialects, religious practices and myths. The climate and soil determined what food could be grown and, from this, distinct cuisines emerged. Shelter and clothes were designed in response to climate and available materials. These cultural basics remained stable elements for countless generations. Even today they regulate how reality is interpreted and how life should be lived.

Cultural distinctions are as much a part of who we are as such core human emotions as jealousy, joy, anguish and love. But there's nothing static about cultures, they are forever evolving and blending. Globalisation – travel, trade, communication, the internet – has taken a toll on uniqueness on every continent. But there is a strong pushback too, against homogenisation as communities identify and seek to preserve their distinctive characteristics and heritage.

It doesn't matter if we personally never witness the Iranian dramatic storytelling Naqqāli, or the United Arab Emirates' traditional weaving skills, Al Sadu. They are invaluable heritage treasures worthy of safeguarding because they make our world more wonderous and celebrate humanity's creative abundance.

A beautiful melding

In Norway, I went to look at a 13ᵗʰ century stave church.
These medieval Christian churches are elegant timber structures,
shaped like upturned boats. By luck, there was a wedding on the day
of our visit. The Norwegian groom and his family wore traditional green
and russet bunad that blended with the surroundings. The Indian bride
and her family wore their national dress, the women's saris bright
as gemstones amongst the pines and dark timbers of the church.
The merging of differences magnified the beauty.

New influences

*Multi*culturalism works when cultural diversity and national community are
in harmony. Not just between those individuals, born here or elsewhere but
between all the various groups. Pakistani influencing Chinese influencing
Italian influencing Mexican. This is the hybridity that immigration creates.
Not us and them, but all of us with something new and vibrant emerging
from the mix.

To flourish, multiculturalism needs places that encourage people
from different backgrounds to congregate and interact. Sport, university
campuses, city streets, cafés, markets and fairs: these are spaces when
we gather effortlessly together, sharing the same commonplace purposes.
To play, to shop, to eat, to learn, to enjoy.

On summer's nights in cities from London to Berlin, Seattle to Brussels,
markets come alive with hawkers, vendors and food trucks selling street
food. The smoke from roasting meat hangs in the warm air; bands pump
out music. There's a mouth-watering array of cuisines: Filipino, Asian,
African, Spanish, Portuguese, Israeli, Greek. It's all colour and noise,
crowds and aromas. People from all walks of life flock to enjoy this
multifarious feast of the senses.

It's hard to maintain disdain for strangers when we sit down with them to share good food and good conversation. We soon forget all notions of other and become – simply, wonderfully – us.

Break down barriers

The aromas and the hubbub at the Moroccan Soup Bar,
run by the amazing Hana Assafiri, transport diners out of Melbourne's
inner-north and into the heart of Marrakesh. Hana encourages frank,
honest dialogue at a monthly Speed Date a Muslim event held at her café.
Diners come specifically to talk to Muslim women about anything that
intrigues, puzzles or unsettles – provided the questions are in good faith.

It's hard to maintain disdain for strangers when we sit down with
them to share good food and good conversation. We soon forget
all notions of other and become – simply, wonderfully – *us*.
Such interaction is a powerful way to break down barriers and
expose the absurdity of stereotypes. We encounter customs,
not as tourism sideshows, but as everyday live reality.

Join the party

On the tram, I eavesdrop on a conversation between two young women.
Speaking in their Australian accents they are talking about the Polish
festival that they had attended the day before. A small, beguiling snapshot
of multiculturalism.

The Polish Festival is one of thousands of community celebrations in
Australia, one of hundreds of thousands around the world, that showcase
food, faith, crafts, dance, song and games. The hugely popular Notting Hill
Carnival in London celebrates West Indian culture. Toronto's Global Festival
brings together a large number of multicultural communities.

Such festivals demonstrate a community's pride in its heritage and invite understanding through the sheer joy of festive fun. They demonstrate common ground (we all love a party) and explain customs (how we party in different ways). They are the glue that binds people across cultures, that cements healthy, mixed societies.

They go a long way to replacing travel. The J-pop Summit in San Francisco exhibits everything Japanese from fashion to tech-innovations to niche subcultures. Germany's iconic Oktoberfest turns up in Brazil, Argentina, China, Canada and elsewhere.

There are numerous festivals that bring the arts in all of their variety to our shores: fringe, film, literature, music, comedy, folk and every other celebratory aspect of life. They introduce multiple aspects of different cultures into our lives in both meaningful and entertaining ways.

The annual Edinburgh International Festival is a good example of the influence of festivals. The main event might be the very homegrown Royal Edinburgh Military Tattoo with its massed bagpipes and drums and other traditional Scottish performances in the shadow of Edinburgh Castle. But the overall atmosphere is definitely cosmopolitan.

People from across the globe flock to Edinburgh to enjoy entertainment that has been sourced from across the globe. The quietly elegant city overflows and becomes exuberantly outward-looking. For the locals, it's a chance to rub shoulders with many different cultures while staying put.

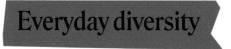

Everyday diversity

In many cities around the world, host communities are so overwhelmed by the volume of tourists that they hide their lives behind closed doors. As visitors, the reality of a place is often shielded from our view. But in our neighbourhood, if we are fortunate enough to share the streets with people from diverse backgrounds, our ordinary everyday interactions with various ways of life are entirely authentic. We buy food from each other, teach children and provide healthcare. We're all just the locals getting on with our lives and each other.

Of course, getting to know the members of our local Pakistani community is not the same as visiting Lahore. In that beautiful, sophisticated city, thousands of years old, the culture has been laid down like sediment, found in everything that can be touched, breathed and tasted.

But we can learn to adjust our sights and our needs – instead of Lahore, local. We can bundle up all of the expectations we would have taken to a foreign city and go looking for what is thriving in our neighbourhood. A festival that celebrates the customs; a Pashtun café serving kabuli palaw and chapli kabab; a sitar-playing busker. We can watch the film *Maula Jatt*. We can read *Mottled Dawn* by Saadat Hasan Manto or *The Wandering Falcon* by Jamil Ahmed.

At home, we can welcome newcomers into our midst. We have the time to engage meaningfully and openly, to use communication to build lasting social bonds. We can research the culture and perhaps a little of the language of our immigrant neighbours as a starting point for building understanding and friendship. From such friendships, we can learn far more about a foreign country than our travel experiences are likely to reveal.

How places evolve

We can turn a corner and enter a different country: strange clothes, language, smells, shops. Even the bustle of daily life can seem alien. For me, all it took was a brisk twelve-minute train ride. Stepping out of the carriage was like stepping into a foreign land.

Footscray is home to the Aboriginal Woiwurrung and Boon Wurrung peoples of the Kulin nation. Through the 19th and 20th centuries the population became dominated by white, working-class families living in a suburb shrouded in industrial pollution. Through further transitions, it now ranks in the top fifty coolest suburbs in the world – which doesn't surprise the locals. Wave after wave of immigrants – first British and European, then Chinese, Vietnamese and Indian, then East African – have instilled Footscray with its own idiosyncratic character. Each group has stamped its distinctiveness, embroidering and infusing the suburb with a diverse and fascinating new identity.

There's a large mural of local Sicilian, Franco Cozzo. Directly opposite the railway station is the Footscray market, famous for its banh mi peddlers. The streets around the market are crowded with African, Vietnamese, Middle Eastern, Italian and Australian eateries.

There's plenty of community pride, especially for the Asylum Seeker Resource Centre and the Footscray Community Arts Centre. Nothing's pretentious. Footscray is simply what it is: a multilayered, multicultural community bursting with life. Like so many suburbs in so many places, it is the sum of all the people who live there.

We can spin a globe, close our eyes and place a finger anywhere, then go in search of the culture we've pointed to. Only, don't book a flight, hit the streets of home.

Inherent kindness

In the summer of 2020, bushfires ravaged the region in which I live. Many people were evacuated from their towns and could not know if the fires had destroyed their homes. Large relief centres were set up to accommodate these anxious souls and to help them through a terrifying time.

Within a few days, members of the Melbourne-based Sikh Volunteers Australia were travelling throughout the fire-affected region, dishing up free food. Undeterred by the thick smoke and confusion, they set about serving hundreds of meals of vegetable curry and rice: warm, comforting food for the fire-weary and distressed. The locals called them legends.

During the COVID-19 lockdowns, Sikh communities fed hungry, isolated families in countries across the globe. The care, charity and kindness of the Sikhs, the gratitude and respect of the recipients: here was bonding that transcended cultural differences and showed that we truly were all in this together.

Places where we flourish

'Everybody needs beauty as well as bread, places to play in and pray in, where Nature may heal and cheer and give strength to body and soul alike.'

John Muir

Hankering for green

Today, more than half of the world's population lives in cities where small apartments prevail and the view is of other buildings and asphalt. It's only natural that, come holiday-time, we should want to turn our backs on the concrete jungle and renew ourselves in nature.

The problem is, we think we have to travel great distances to find true nature. Off we go to earth's last great wilderness – us and hundreds of thousands of others. It takes a fair degree of wilful blindness to ignore the way in which our travels to untamed frontiers hasten destruction and extinction.

Being at one with the natural world is vital to our wellbeing – we are a part of it and it's where we belong. But like so much else, it's about where we find it and how we experience it.

Citizen scientists

Ordinary people have long helped scientists informally to monitor wildlife and collect data. Now Citizen Science has become a formally organised, world-wide programme of people contributing to scientific research and knowledge.

It might begin with a local group suggesting an idea to scientists, or it might be that scientists need people on the ground to collect specific information. Kids collecting insects in the backyard, birders and WeatherBugs, social clubs, and mums and dads worried about the future. However and whoever, it's collaborative and worthwhile, bringing together people who share a love and concern for the natural world and who are keen to advance our protection of it. It makes a worthwhile staycation activity.

Natural therapy

Shinrin-yoku loosely translated from Japanese means forest bathing – strolling through nature without intentions. It is a form of soft fascination that leaves our minds free to wander, to be soothed by all that is around us. To watch the clouds and dappled light. To listen to the birds, insects, and the breeze. To feel the texture of bark and moss, the tackiness of sap. To smell the spiciness of leaves after rain. To taste the fresh air.

Being outside in a natural environment is therapeutic for both body and mind. Recognising this, national parks around the world have adopted the motto 'Healthy Parks, Healthy People' to highlight the connectivity between parks, people and the wellbeing of both.

Closed to commercial development, national parks not only preserve ecosystems, they also preserve the past, telling their own form of travel stories back into deep history. The first national park, Yellowstone, was created in 1872. Even then, preserving tracts of land as cultural resources for future generations was deemed vital. Today, there are over 4000 national parks in the world, telling every possible story about place.

We can visit national parks in other countries to be awed and informed, but they are never anything other than foreign places. Only in our own national parks can we connect personally to the elements of landscape, flora and fauna. We can trace geomorphological beginnings, cultural practices of the earliest inhabitants and changes wrought by evolving social and political thinking. Sadly, we can also see how environments are being reshaped by climate change. These are the chronicles that not only define a country's distinctive landscape but its people's character too. Think of the difference between Uluru in the Australian outback and Canada's Banff National Park.

By getting to know *our* national sites of natural and cultural significance we shore up the stories that bind us to the place where we belong. They contribute to our sense of place, they are part of who we are. There's therapy in this, too.

Uncover perfection

Some places are so exceptional that it simply isn't possible to find equivalents at home. For me, Saihoji Temple near Kyoto is one such place. The Zen Buddhist temple, established over 1200 years ago, is set in a vast ancient garden of aching beauty. Lush moss covers everything, giving the place its popular name Kokedera, meaning Moss Temple.

After a religious ritual in the Hondo, I applied myself to a calligraphy lesson, sitting seiza-style and copying expressive Sanskrit characters. Only when I had slowed down and entered the right frame of mind was I released into the gardens.

A path wound through the Karesansui rock and stone garden, and on to the classical garden where the leaves were turning, their colours as rich as royal gowns. Past the Ougonchi pond in the shape of a heart and the tea house with its moon-watching area. Monks silently gathered leaves as they fell.

The walk was a true shinrin-yoku experience, before I knew the term. We emerged from the garden spellbound and carried our silence all the way back to Kyoto.

Perfection, yes ... and yet. On a recent walk, near my home, I came across a huge cobweb, sunshine catching rows of dew drops, turning them into tiny prisms of colour. Long, long gossamer threads anchored the cobweb to a bush, a bare branch high overhead, and a clump of sedge. What magic the spider had spun. Here was wondrous nature – mysterious and beautiful – five minutes from my house.

On the box

We don't have to fly to faraway places to see extraordinary natural wonders – David Attenborough has been bringing them into our homes for decades. We can follow him around the globe exploring remote locations and spying on creatures we would never in a lifetime see, no matter how much we've travelled. The most astonishing, remotest places; the most incredible sights; the most bizarre animal behaviour: all there for us to enjoy without adding one extra carbon footprint.

Nature on our doorstep

If we actively look about our neighbourhood, be it inner city, suburban or country town, we can find pockets of greenspace. From parklands to home gardens, street planting to wild creepers along railway cuttings or riverbanks. Restauranteurs are growing vegetables and herbs, apartment dwellers are planting gardens on rooftops. Biophilic design has entered the urban-planning lexicon. Urban forests have become a focus as studies show that heavily treed urban areas can store as much carbon per hectare as tropical rainforests.

If we have a space, creating a garden links us to place, sending down deep roots of belonging. A home garden is a sanctuary, a hobby, a release for our creative urges, a place to play. It might be considered a trivial pastime, and our daffodils are not going to feed the world, but they do feed our human desire for beauty. The beauty we create contributes, simply, preciously, to our contentment.

It is a place of slow time where we can witness daily how nature works. We learn the deliberate, patterned ways of the creatures who visit, the plants as they grow.

The same witnessing of nature can take place at the local park, regardless of whether it is as grand as London's Hyde Park or just a humble little patch of green. Any place where we can direct our gaze, perhaps for the first time, towards all of nature's shades of green. To watch as the rising sun crowns the trees in golden light. To follow a bee as it distributes pollen from one flower to the next.

Botanic gardens are in a league of their own. More than public parks and gardens, they are essentially scientific sites for the study of plants. Indeed, botanic gardens are the oldest scientific institutions in the world. The first, the Orto botanico di Pisa, appeared in Italy in 1544. London's famous Chelsea Physic Garden was founded in 1673 in association with the Worshipful Society of Apothecaries for the study of medicinal plants. These days botanic gardens are found in almost every major city in the developed world from Singapore to Morocco. Their principle role remains largely unchanged from those earliest beginnings: to conserve plants through research and to study habitats. They are also living museums: the keepers of historically important and geographically diverse collections.

When we step into our local botanic garden, we enter a haven, seemingly a million miles from the city clamour just beyond its boundaries. This living laboratory is ideal for staycations, offering a place to relax and feast the eye. It is for plant lovers and for children to run and explore. A place for weddings, theatrical performances or movies under the stars. It's a city sanctuary for wildlife and birdlife. There are shrubs and trees to see, smell and touch. The lawn is cool and green, the lakes mirror the trees and sky, the flowers are an artist's palette.

A trip to the nursery

Plant nurseries are places of living loveliness. Suburban oases, they offer an easy passage into plant life in all of its variety and splendour. There, we buy compost and watering systems as foundations for the beauty we hold in our mind's eye. We read labels and matchmake shrubs to spots in the garden. We linger over lush indoor greenery and punnets of vegetable seedlings. We take home more than we had planned, unable to resist the flowering clematis or bag of tulip bulbs. Surely, this is one of the most uplifting forms of shopping.

Connect, respect, protect

Cape Conran Coastal Park is an hour and a half's drive from where I live. Campsites nestle amongst banksia trees and short paths lead to a broad sweep of beach. I camp there regularly – it's like a second home. I swim, walk, read, body surf, birdwatch and kayak. I spend time there with friends, cooking a shared meal over a campfire and talking late into the night. With no ambient light, the night sky is creamy with stars; the moon so bright we hardly need torches.

It's a magical place, the traditional land of the Krowathunkooloong people, mysterious and ancient. Middens (the original garbage bins, designed for discarding food scraps to prevent littering) dating back 10,000 years provide evidence of long habitation. A land of mild climate, abundant food and fresh water, with reeds to weave baskets, tree bark to build canoes, ochre for ceremonial body decoration. Here, the traditional owners continue to care for the country where they have hunted, feasted, told stories, sung and danced and handed on customs from one generation to the next for eons. Their imprint runs deep and true.

On the Yeerung River we launch our kayaks and paddle upstream – and back in time. Or so it feels. Thickly silent except for birdcalls and the gentle splash of our paddle blades. As the river narrows, we pass through a tunnel of overhanging branches and navigate around moss-covered snags.

The sense of place we experience at Cape Conran derives from a feeling of merging with the environment and being attuned to the reverberations of ancient times. It's a place to feed the soul, to slow down and pay close attention to the myriad manifestations of the natural world.

It is through our appreciation of and connection to special places like Cape Conran that we comprehend what we stand to lose if we don't act on climate change.

(I wrote this before our summer of 2020, when bushfires ripped through East Gippsland, destroying much of Cape Conran. Personally, it felt like losing a piece of myself. It felt like grief. Like many others, I could not avoid drawing a direct line between greenhouse-gas emissions and the loss of this ancient beauty. We can't save the precious places close to home without taking action to save the planet.)

It is through our appreciation of and connection to special places like Cape Conran that we comprehend what we stand to lose if we don't act on climate change.

Urban explorer

'The whole object of travel is not to set foot on foreign land; it is at last to set foot on one's own country as a foreign land'.

G.K. Chesterton

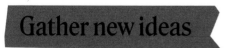

Gather new ideas

I've known Melbourne all my life. The laneways, cafés, theatres and shops; the buskers, bookshops and trams. Or at least I thought I knew the city until I visited the Melbourne Visitor Hub (the tourist information centre). There, I was introduced to another Melbourne entirely full of hidden gems. Not touristy places but real-life stuff – a cul-de-sac of craft shops, a quirky bar, extraordinary architecture, small specialist museums. Gritty and glamorous, everyday and exceptional – so many places that I never knew existed. Had I been walking around with my eyes closed all these years?

City or country, we overlook our local tourist information centre as a resource *for us*. We might go to get ideas for visiting friends and relatives, but heck, this is home. They're just for the tourists, right? Wrong. Tourist information centres are staffed by people who have made it their profession to know their city more exhaustively than most of its inhabitants. These experts not only have insider information, they have infectious enthusiasm.

It's the same with sightseeing buses, river cruises, or walking tours. Why leave them solely to visitors when they, too, can reveal aspects of our city we've always overlooked? A cruise along Melbourne's Yarra River gave me my first real appreciation of the extensive dock activity that makes Victoria tick.

With great anticipation, I unfold a map for a self-guided walking tour that I picked up at the Melbourne Visitor Hub. It's a guide to the city's street art. I could have selected parklands or Aboriginal heritage or cathedrals or a music walk or a loop around bookshops and libraries.

Once again, I am confounded by how little I know of *my* city. Street art is something I've walked past without it catching my interest. The map leads me into laneways I've never walked down, past old buildings which I didn't know still existed. I discover hidden bars and cafés, patches of thriving greenery and remnants of Melbourne's mercantile past. And everywhere, the walls are alive with bold figures and bizarre creatures in colours that swirl and zigzag and practically twang. There are protest slogans and pop stars and climbing plants with big trumpet flowers. Taking time to stop, I think about what I can see. What is the message the artist wants to convey? Will it even be here next week? Suddenly, street art is no longer something I want to ignore.

Art on the streets

Street art comes out of a long legacy of public art, beginning with cave paintings. Throughout history, it has documented the times politically and socially. These days, there's global cross-pollination and a universal street-art language. Groups of international street artists travel the world at the invitation of councils and corporations, to brighten up decaying neighbourhoods and ugly buildings. The mysterious Banksy is world renowned. The French artist JR calls himself an artivist, combining the dual roles of artist and activist.

It's the subcultural nature of the art that keeps it edgy. It rebels against the highbrow. It is free to view and to touch. It is wild, creative, derivative, ugly, colourful, surreal, dynamic. It challenges what is public and what is private; what is legal and what is criminal. It's collaborative and helps artists develop their individual styles. Its transience adds urgency. It's playful and energetic, or it's demonic and demanding, or fun and meaningless. It's in-your-face or hidden away. It's mediocre or highly accomplished.

As a genre that explores cultural identity, disrupts our notions of art and attacks complacency it's worth our attention. It contributes to our sense of place.

Observe beauty ...

In 1986, the architectural historian Terunobu Fujimori helped found the Japanese Street Observation Society. The society brings together people who scour city streets for beauty, oddities and humour in overlooked places and objects. Fujimori named the practice Rojo Kansatsu. Rojo means a sense of passing through, Kansatsu means observation. His followers forge beyond the obvious, to uncover such whimsy as tsuboniwa or spot gardens. These might be small patches of grass growing in roadway cracks, a pillow of moss on a wall, a pattern of pebbles or tiny plants in the indents of a manhole cover. Fujimori says that when we find something good, it gives us feelings of freedom and ownership.

On Melbourne's main downtown intersection, we have to look up to see the weathervanes mounted high on tram poles. One on each of the four corners, there's a horse, a pig, a fish and a bird, made of hand-beaten copper with gold leaf detail. There above our heads, they perform an aerial dance with each gust of wind. The sculptor, Daniel Jenkins, wants people to look up and smile.

... and harmony

Placemaking is what urban planners do to bring strangers together harmoniously. Urban designs take into account the multiple, intertwined layers of everyday human activity – physical, cultural, social and ecological. They recognise that place is more than just the locality where we live and work. It's *how* we live with each other. When places function well, they promote tolerance and diversity through a sense of shared identity and social experience.

During the COVID-19 lockdown, we witnessed countless acts of innovative, grassroots placemaking. A yoga teacher offered lessons from her front yard to neighbours in their front yards. People stood at their front doors and banged pots to show thanks to health workers. In Florence, the opera singer Maurizio Marchini sang *Nessun Dorma* from his balcony. The neighbours loved it, the YouTube video went viral. Professional placemakers would never have imagined such ingenious ways of connecting.

The author and activist Jane Jacobs was an early proponent of placemaking, believing cities were about people, not buildings. Every public space should bustle with civic life, and every street frontage should be active. Jacobs fought against the 1960s mania for leveling vast swathes of vibrant neighbourhoods, reducing lively mixed communities to silent, gentrified monocultures.

Spots in time

A friend writes to me of what he calls spots in time: serendipitous encounters while travelling overseas. One was a totally unexpected and exquisite performance of water puppets in Hanoi. In Copenhagen, it was stumbling across a performance of Verdi's *Requiem* in a small traditional church in the old city, on a cold and otherwise silent evening. The atmosphere of the old church majestically and uniquely transformed the familiar music.

Extraordinary spots in time, outside what's promoted and pre-planned, can be found anywhere. We can be charmed and surprised – every day.

At home I watched a young man on a skateboard being towed along by his dog while he nonchalantly sipped coffee. And walking past the lawn forecourt of Melbourne's Art Centre, I noticed actors from the Bell Shakespeare Company had invited ordinary people to act out *Romeo and Juliet*. The young boy randomly chosen to play Romeo had stardom written all over him.

A slow pace, not a race

Our walking pace of 5 kilometres (3 miles) per hour, the Danish architect Jan Gehl observes, spawns slow architecture rich in detail – the fine detail of those colourful Dublin doors is only noticeable on slow-paced inspection. Car travel, at 60 kilometres (40 miles) per hour, fosters fast architecture resulting in boring, featureless buildings.

Being alert to the distinction between slow and fast architecture can help us to decide where we want to explore, and what we might look out for. Rhythm and scale, light and space, colour and movement, variety and detail. These are the elements that absorb us as urban explorers.

When hunting for the unusual, we often limit our sight to the ground floor of buildings and pay scant attention to what happens up above. What a shame to only see half the story. In this age of global brands with shopfronts the same the world over, the street level is rarely unique. Upstairs, above the verandahs, awnings and plate-glass windows is where the past lives on, where we can discover originality and traditional style.

City skylines have a beauty, in their jumbled mix of building profiles, of different textures, colours and heights. Massed communication aerials, radio masts and satellite dishes turn rooftops into space stations. The sheer glass facades of modern skyscrapers mirror the sky: clouds dance across their surface, the setting sun turns them molten gold. Find a bench and sit for a while to watch this light show in the sky.

We might even venture inside, into foyers that often house spectacular artwork. Public art in essence, but rarely seen by the public. It deserves our attention, along with the interior design. Our interest piqued, we might make a note to take part in the next Open House weekend – an initiative that happens annually in over forty cities around the world. The objective is to open our eyes to our hometown architecture, to learn about the importance of good design and to stimulate community debate about future developments.

Country towns have their own charms worth exploring. Many historical societies conduct guided tours, offer self-guided walking maps or downloadable apps. Their commentary can be so informed and broad ranging that it fills in previously unknown backstories about the place we may have lived all of our lives. Heritage sites, cemeteries, parks, notable citizens' homes and public buildings all have their histories to tell, their secrets to reveal.

The sheer glass facades of modern skyscrapers mirror the sky: clouds dance across their surface, the setting sun turns them molten gold. Find a bench and sit for a while to watch this light show in the sky.

Cities and towns can be fun. There is plenty to amuse us if we are in the right frame of mind.

Cities and towns can be fun. There is plenty to amuse us if we are in the right frame of mind. There might be a sign with an unintended meaning, an oddly shaped tree, advertisements that make outrageous claims, quirky sculptures and comic street art, a parade of preening pigeons. Look for juxtapositions such as an incongruously located little shop, bright with life, in a line of ugly edifices. A friend sent me a photo he'd taken outside the Art Gallery of Ballarat – a regional gallery with a fine permanent collection and international-class exhibitions. Parked in front of the gallery was a truck advertising horse dentistry.

Agents of change

Who would have thought something so mundane as a shipping container could revolutionise construction? Originally an idea to reduce handling costs and theft, shipping containers led to the obsolescence of every upstream dock, wharf and warehouse in the world. In turn, these abandoned spaces evolved into other purposes. London's Canary Wharf became the city's second financial centre.

After the 2011 Christchurch earthquake shipping containers were used as barriers to protect houses, vehicles and pedestrians from falling rocks and debris; as supports for badly damaged buildings, as temporary sheds and shelters for workers. They were used with great flair to create a mini downtown of innovative pop-up shops and cafés.

Elsewhere, there's a growing trend to repurpose these big metal boxes for permanent homes and even hotels: sustainability at its most innovative, detached from their history.

Part two

Worlds within worlds

Cultural connections

*'A nation's culture resides in the hearts and
in the soul of its people.'*

Mahatma Gandhi

How we belong

Far more than travel, learning about the culture to which we belong helps us
find ourselves and our place in the world. Our culture is an expression of who
we are and how we choose to live. It showcases what we value as a society
and how we make sense of what is around us. Our culture belongs to us and
is part of us residing, as Gandhi says, in our heart and soul. That alone
makes it profoundly special.

Our cultural organisations and institutions take us on amazing journeys
into the heart of the place to which we belong. Reflecting our culture through
stories, paintings, music, history, drama and writing, they celebrate the
best of us. They verify that humans are capable of so much imagination,
creativity, inventiveness and splendour. By questioning society's
conventions, they encourage us to question, too. There's more insight and
truth in what they offer us than we will ever glean from all of our skimming
voyages across the earth's surface.

There's so much to be experienced at very little or no cost. From opera
to hip-hop, the arts are delivered into our homes via Spotify and YouTube.
There are small-town theatre productions and buskers on street corners;

local enthusiasts exhibiting their collections of cars or fountain pens; regional historical societies and private gardens open to the public; heritage-listed country manors and war memorials. They all contribute to the cultural mix that reveals to us who we are and how we connect to place.

Sport is as much culture as theatre, expressing a society's values, beliefs and ideals. Stadiums evolve into cultural icons. Games encourage social interaction and break down differences and prejudices. The local football club is often a community's cultural glue.

Culture isn't one thing. It's everything. It is us, all of *us*, at every level.

Cultural revelations

Communities reveal themselves through cultural events, big and small. On a very cold and wet day in Wales, we went along to a local agricultural show (oh, the mud!). It was so down-to-earth, so *honest* in its representations of what mattered to the locals, that we felt that we had been given a unique insight into that Welsh farming community's culture. A similar event held annually in my local area provides a confirmation of what I think I know about our farming community's ways of life and work. It also surprises and delights with new revelations.

So much easier than a long-haul flight,
our quest for meaning can draw us
into the worlds of art, music, drama, history
and literature that exist all around us.

Curiosity, wonder and culture

Curiosity is the keenness to learn about ourselves and our world based on the two questions central to our existence – *why* and *how*. It is at the core of our search for meaning in life. To be curious about our own culture is to embark on a life-expanding journey. In turn, our cultural investigations sharpen and refine our curiosity. This closed loop keeps us exploring.

So much easier than a long-haul flight, our quest for meaning can draw us into the worlds of art, music, drama, history and literature that exist all around us. We discover that the arts in all of its manifestations can satisfy many of the reasons we use to justify our globetrotting ways.

We might think we need the jolt of travel to spark our curiosity, the answers to *why* and *how* relying on the stimulus of unfamiliar settings. But it's at home, where the quest is intimately connected to self, that we find answers that are closest to our heart.

Wonder, an extension of curiosity, takes us into the realms of the uncanny. Unlike curiosity, we don't expect answers to our wonder questions. While we love the adventure curiosity entails – chasing answers, the buzz of success – we also love the elusiveness of things beyond our grasp. We thrill in what haunts us. That musical phrase that seems to speak to something deep inside us; the small bronze sculpture that captivates us without us understanding why. This is wonder at work. How and why we become deeply attached to the place we call home holds its own mystery. That makes our explorations into our own culture all the more engaging.

How familiarity helps

Travelling to get a taste of other ways of life is interesting, but in unfamiliar situations, when time is limited and the language foreign, our heads spin with questions, but the answers are often elusive. Even our searches for detailed information on the internet and in guidebooks can deaden rather than enliven our curiosity.

Familiarity may dampen our curiosity, but it can also help. If we sharpen our curiosity locally and re-examine what we thought we knew, the questions that arise are relatively easy to answer and understand. New insights link all the scraps of information we have unconsciously absorbed. Familiarity makes a strong platform from which to expand our horizons.

How and why we become deeply attached to the place we call home holds its own mystery. That makes our explorations into our own culture all the more engaging.

The arts make us whole

As doors closed during the COVID-19 pandemic, the arts community
opened its heart to lift our spirits. If there was ever a doubt about the
importance of the arts, it was banished during our long days of self-isolation.
The internet lit up with everything from virtual museum tours, to ask-a-librarian
pages, to online art gallery exhibitions, to musicians of every genre
connecting us through music and song.

For many weeks, my Fridays revolved around a night at the theatre.
From London, the National Theatre streamed sixteen productions, and on
the opposite side of the world, we dressed up, poured glasses of wine, and
settled down for a world-class performance. We were just one of nine million
households across one hundred and seventy-three countries grateful to the
National Theatre for lightening our days and enriching our lives.

We discovered how the arts keep us sane. We need to hold on
to that idea through whatever the future has in store. Art in all its forms
is a haven, capable of lifting us out of ourselves and our troubles
into a positive, enlarging place.

Stages of the journey

*'I regard the theatre as the greatest of all art forms, the most
immediate way in which a human being can share with another
the sense of what it is to be a human being.'*

Oscar Wilde

Suspend disbelief

The curtain rises and the buzz becomes a hush. There is a collective intake
of air, as if this is the last breath we will take in the real world for some time
to come. For we are no longer in a theatre on a particular day. We travel to
wherever the story takes us in space and time. For as long as the play lasts,
we will believe without question in this make-believe world.

Theatre people speak of suspending belief. When the story is true to life
and every character on stage seems as real as the person sitting next to us,
we want to treasure the illusions, not dispute them.

Ways of telling

Millions of people travel around the world to visit war memorials. In these often
tranquil settings, restraint amplifies the atrocity and injustice of war. While
war memorials can be profound expressions of forgiveness and hope, they are
so sobering and overwhelming that it can be difficult to know how to respond.

There is, however, a low-carbon alternative. A play can tell the story of
war in ways that animate, decipher and intensify what war memorials seek

to convey. By laying out before us the impact on individual lives – played by living actors – the drama helps us to respond in ways that feel right.

In Michael Morpurgo's play *Warhorse* it takes only a few props to transport us to the countryside in Devon, England, or onto a battlefield in France. We quickly forget that the foal Joey is a cane frame covered with cloth, visibly controlled by puppeteers. The puppetry does nothing to diminish the truth of the story about the brutality and senselessness of war. Our response to the horror is no less genuine and likely more understandable, than what we experience when we visit sites such as the Hiroshima Peace Memorial Park in Japan or the war cemeteries of France and Belgium.

No cameras allowed

The ban on cameras in theatres means that we don't dilute the experience of live performance by seeing it through a lens. A photo might certify that we were there, but it's a souvenir rather than a palpable, rewarding experience. When we become absorbed in a play, the complexities and morals of the story enter our subconscious, there to be drawn upon whenever and wherever we need help to interpret the world.

There is a time and a place for the perfect Instagram shot, but it is important to remember there are still experiences that offer something so memorable that they stay in the mind, not on the phone.

Honest portrayals

Plays offer something for everyone, at every level, of every interest. We go to see *Nine Night* to witness what it is like to be caught between two cultures, or *What the Constitution Means to Me* to be informed in a way that offers light relief from often hostile arguments. We go to any of Shakespeare's plays because we read them at school and want to see them brought to life. We go for the mastery of the actors, the glamour of the venue and the opportunity to dress up.

Whatever our reason, the play we see will falter if it fails to tell the truth. It will fail if it tries to fake it. Good plays, whether tragedy or comedy, assume that we are intelligent and empathetic. Theatre and travel might overlap in the way that both expose us to how others live, causing us to reflect on our own ways. But as revealing as our travels may be, they rarely expose us to anything as complex and truthful as Hamlet's anguished attempt to unravel the purpose of life.

So much of tourism is confected, bending the truth in varying degrees to supply entertainment more than enlightenment. While Hiroshima Peace Memorial Park is so nakedly honest it takes our breath away, tourists also flock to see Juliet's balcony (from *Romeo and Juliet*) in Verona. They willingly believe it's the real thing, even though Juliet was a figment of Shakespeare's imagination and there's no mention of a balcony in the play.

On the stage, even though there's no question that Romeo and Juliet are fictional, we don't doubt the truthfulness in Shakespeare's portrayal of their love and grief. Written more than 400 years ago, the play's honesty makes it timeless and universal.

It's this theatrical sincerity that sustains our attention, in the moment and afterwards. We can stand before the world's grandest monuments or sweeping vistas and after a short while our minds will start to wander. We think about where we'll have lunch, or look about for a patch of shade, or check what time the bus leaves. We might even ask ourselves, *is that all there is?* Whereas good, honest theatre captivates. Our attention never strays, everything in the play is important and has something vital to tell us. We must see it through to the end.

A journey into the heart

Theatre can take us anywhere, on a journey far beyond the material world, into the human mind and heart. We make the journey any time. We can weave theatre into our lives in a way that travel does not allow.

Theatre venues are places of bonding, where actors and audience breathe the same air. The audience participates by being there. Within 5–10 minutes of a play beginning, people who don't know each other begin to react as one being. The actors on stage are as influenced by the reactions of the audience as the audience is transported by the skill of the actors. No two performances are ever the same and unpredictability generates its own excitement.

The finest plays sustain cultures; they also transcend them. *The Doll's House*, *Death of a Salesman*, *Saigon*, these are universal stories that extend far beyond the country and circumstances in which they originated. Whether they are staged by a world-class repertory company, the local theatre group or our kids' school, the value of the message remains unchanged.

New plays enter the culture to help define who we are at this moment in time. Old plays are reworked, their timeless messages subtly brought up to date to keep the stories fresh and relevant. In Australia, the Bell Shakespeare Company cast Kate Mulvany as Richard III. Without altering the script, the play pointed to contemporary debates about gender, misogyny and disability.

Plays can become cultural icons. Agatha Christie's whodunit *The Mousetrap* is as British and unvarying as the Changing of the Guard at Buckingham Palace. The play ran continuously from 1952 until 2020, when the pandemic closed it down. Although it has been a tourist attraction, the majority of the audience was always British. This often is the case: we want to see plays that impart a particular truth about us. Plays which originate in different countries, translated into our own language, give us a glimpse into the nuances of different cultures and help us to think about issues from alternative perspectives.

A play can be comic and light, it can be heartbreaking, political, satirical, subversive or uncomfortable. In tragedy, the story is disturbing and ends badly. We leave the theatre with our heads full of questions about the worst and best of human behaviour.

Fun in lockdown

Humour helps us to bond. We don't only laugh at the antics on stage, we take joy in laughing along with our fellow theatregoers. When the theatres closed and we entered hibernation, YouTube lit up with funny little moments of theatre to amuse us and lighten our days. We quickly shared the videos with friends and family. This form of homegrown theatre helped to see us through. Laughter relaxes, but it's one thing to laugh alone, and another, completely, to share the laughter with others.

Comedies are far less demanding and have happy endings. In plays like *The Importance of Being Ernest*, the deceptions and conflicts are there for our amusement, although they still offer insights into human nature. We laugh our way through the action and leave the theatre with a new lightness in our step. For days afterwards, moments come back to us and we chuckle anew.

Whatever the theme, theatre has the power to provoke conversations that blossom into broader discussions about how we want to live – what to cherish, what to change. Playwrights unpick major contemporary concerns to help us understand their complexities. *On the Beach* and *Resilience* are two plays by British playwright Steve Waters that tackle climate change. *Refugee Boy* is another play that lays bare for us a contemporary conundrum.

The pandemic caused such a disruption to our lives, but it also gave us time to reflect on what we want from life. What will be our new normal? Politicians will give us one answer, based on the economy; sociologists another based on social structure. Travel won't answer much at all. It will be the arts that carve out a broader scope of enquiry. New ideas will emphasise our changed needs. Before our eyes, actors will make sense of the chaos and unfurl new possibilities of being.

Take a trip to the movies

Live theatre and cinema are similar in some respects. Both have actors, scripts and scenes, but movies are very much their own artform.

Filmmakers gather up all of the arts – literature, photography, music and opera. Every frame is a painting, every dramatic moment enhanced by music, every spoken word the art of a dramatist. It covers an amazingly wide scope, from low-budget horror movies to arthouse masterpieces.

Films are the end product of multiple takes and copious editing, striving for perfection that once finalised remains locked in its own time, unlike theatre where each performance is unique.

During the time we were closeted with our various small screens, movies kept us entertained, amused, distracted, thoughtful and rational. But while settling down to watch Netflix in our slippers is very pleasant, there's something special about going out to the cinema. The shared space, the darkness, the big screen (the popcorn). It's an atmosphere just like the theatre where strangers share an experience. At the end of the film, especially a deeply moving story, there's a palpable sense of shared emotion as we emerge blinking into the light of the real world.

Cinemas can be found in the most unlikely of places, from rooftops to parks to floating on harbours. The settings become part of the enchantment of watching movies old and new. Wherever we watch them, movies expand our horizons. On the screen, we get to see inside private houses, we see people at work and war, we journey across magnificent landscapes, we witness how characters respond to situations within their cultural and generational paradigms. And because movies so effortlessly exploit time, we gain an impression of a place through every season, every upheaval.

We can learn more in a few hours spent watching a foreign-language movie than we'll glean from a short stay in a foreign city. As the filmmaker Bong Joon Ho said, 'Once you overcome the one-inch tall barrier of subtitles you will be introduced to so many more amazing films'. Without, we might add, overwhelming host communities in our efforts to understand how they see the world.

Watching *Roma*, *The Body Remembers When the World Broke Open* or *Samson and Delilah* exposes the rawness of marginalised Indigenous communities. *Woman at War* gives us passage to Iceland. *Everybody Knows* illuminates a very human dimension of Spanish family and community life.

All screening at a cinema near home.

Music and the movies

Try watching a segment of a movie where there's no dialogue. Watch it with the sound muted, that is, without the musical accompaniment. Then watch it with the soundtrack and notice how the music intensifies the action. Perhaps the music is needed to convey an atmosphere in films that live actors can create on stage. Whatever the reason, music has always been an essential part of the movie experience. Silent movies were never silent. Anything from a pianist to a whole orchestra played alongside the screen to elaborate on and make sense of what was happening. When Ennio Morricone composed the score for *The Mission*, he wasn't only writing music, he was underpinning the very emotions that would expand our response to the drama.

Cinemas can be found in the most unlikely of places, from rooftops to parks to floating on harbours. The settings become part of the enchantment of watching movies old and new.

Let music transport you

'Music is a moral law. It gives soul to the universe, wings to the mind, flight to the imagination, and charm and gaiety to life and to everything.'

Plato

Discover the world through music

We all love music and are moved by it. It's in our genes, regardless of race, gender, faith or wealth. It's as old as time.

While music is an expression of culture, it is also a language we all understand, a meeting point, a cause for people to come together, to share and learn about each other. It doesn't discriminate, yet it's a fundamental way of celebrating cultural diversity. It requires no passport to cross borders and unite strangers in remarkable ways. No matter what our heritage, we know the difference between a lullaby and a dirge. We all have music for dancing and to mark life's milestones.

Without the need to travel, music introduces us to a world outside our own cultural conventions. It reveals the strangeness, to our ears, of other musical expressions. Just as Queen's *Bohemian Rhapsody* might sound bizarre to the people of the Asian Steppes, Mongolian Khoomei (throat) singing is strange to Western ears.

Venturing beyond our musical boundaries into the unknown is something we can do while remaining at home. We can take a musical tour through our local community hall, school, church, pub, café, botanic garden or winery. We can fire up our iPod, stream from our phone or turn on the radio. From grand concert halls to street corners, people of different backgrounds are making music of every possible genre, for every demographic. It's so readily available, so easily accessed, and as inexpensive as we need it to be. There's no need to trample all over the earth to enjoy the music of the world.

History in tunes

For Indigenous Australians, the world was sung into existence. The songlines that were laid down in ancient times to map the landscape are still in use today. For the Hopi people of North America, life was woven from the threads of songs.

Icelandic folksongs recount tales of elves and trolls, of sailors and harsh winters. Colonisation and slavery in Bolivia produced music that merges Indigenous, Spanish and African styles. The melancholic strains of Portuguese Fado originated in poverty-stricken port towns in the early 1800s. Folk music from rural areas everywhere recounts the turning seasons, the harvest and festivals. And love. Always love. Amongst the ripening corn or behind the bales of hay.

Jazz grew out of African-slave spirituals; flamenco from gypsy tinkers beating time on their pots. Rap and hip-hop existed centuries ago as rhythmic stories told in West Africa and Jamaica, transformed on the streets of New York into electronic compositions.

As with other art forms, music has a way of capturing and interpreting the times. During the Second World War, Vera Lynn sang nostalgically that peace would surely return and couples would meet again, while upbeat sing-alongs helped to lift sagging spirits. John Lennon's *Imagine* – probably the most influential song of all time – was a plea for peace when the nuclear arms race was on everyone's mind. Bob Dylan's poetic lyrics were as topical, intelligent and full of protest against the status quo in the 1960s and '70s as Kendrick Lamar's are now.

An expression of life

Take away our opportunity to travel and we feel disappointed. Take away our chance to make and listen to music and we forsake part of our humanity. Music expresses the wonder of *us*. Physicist Professor Brian Cox linked great classical works to science's explorations through the cosmos. Both ask the question, what does it mean to be human in a seemingly meaningless universe? If there are answers, Cox said, they are to be found in music as well as science.

When music brings us together, we experience what psychologists call emotional contagion. Think of Queen at the 1985 Live Aid concert at Wembley Stadium – 72,000 people joyously singing *We will rock you* along with Freddie Mercury. All those different backgrounds and approaches to life, melded by music, harmonised into one entity.

Join a choir

Monday night, people gather at a Salvation Army Chapel. They come from all walks of life, faiths, abilities. They greet each other as if this were one big family. They've come – these thirty adults ranging from their early twenties to late seventies – for the joy of singing in a choir, for the confidence-building, for the social interaction and support.

The late afternoon sun streams through stained-glass windows; the traffic noise drops away. There's just the song, and the desire to make it as good as possible. We can hear the smiles in the singers' voices. Before long, their bodies are swaying in time. They have come here to find themselves, not through travel but through singing. Not just for a week or two, but for a lifetime. Neuroscientists tell us that singing makes us healthier, happier, smarter and more creative. It nurtures love and compassion, imagination, hope and inspiration. We might feel uplifted when singing alone in the shower or the car but singing in a choir greatly amplifies all the benefits.

Even the COVID-19 pandemic couldn't stop the singing. Pub Choir, that dazzling mix of music, comedy and beer evolved, with the help of some creative technology, into Couch Choir. We raised our voices not in isolated despair but in the euphoric knowledge that we were part of a world-wide, virtual choir. Holidaying at home is the perfect opportunity to join a choir and embrace the joy of singing with others.

Life's soundtrack

Music can instantly draw us back in time, in particular to those intense years of adolescence when individuality and independence take form.

The songs of our youth narrated what we were going through. When we were too timid, confused, uncertain or embarrassed to say how we felt, lyrics articulated our feelings. A song was often the background to our first kiss, our eighteenth birthday, our first car. Popular songs helped us to live through broken hearts and to express our emerging anti-establishment leanings.

Music not only takes us back to those turbulent teenage years, it can transport us anywhere or connect to other sensory memories. For my husband, the *William Tell Overture* is a tenacious link to his birthplace Newcastle Upon Tyne. When I hear *The Skye Boat Song*, I can smell the chalk and wooden desks of my primary school years.

As the years unfold, our musical taste evolves in ways that reflect how we choose to live. Whatever the genre – country music or heavy metal, indie or classical – we never stop turning to music to express our deepest feelings in the ways that feel true to us. That's why it's so important to explore our musical landscape, because it tells us much about ourselves.

Listen for the wonder

Neuroscientists speak of neural circuits and temporal lobes, brain mapping and computer modelling when they address the question, why does music move us? While such scientific language is vitally important to explaining how the brain works, it robs music of its beguiling mystery. It adds nothing to understanding the emotions we feel listening to Beethoven's *Ninth Symphony*. Nor is there any need to ask how one man could create such perfection out of nothing. All that matters is that in this sweep of glory that culminates in the famous *Ode to Joy*, Beethoven gave the world an anthem without borders, music that encapsulates equality, freedom and humanity. Even if we don't understand the German words (from a poem by Friedrich Schiller), the sentiment provoked by chorus and orchestra can move us to tears. Fittingly, this was the music chosen to mark the dismantling of the Berlin Wall.

There's no doubt that travel can yield moments of awe and wonder, from spectacular views to extraordinary architecture to amazing encounters. But we don't have to go far to be stirred so deeply. The experience of awe is there in Allegri's 17th century sacred choral work *Miserere*. This music was once considered so precious that the Catholic Church forbade it from being performed outside the Sistine Chapel. There it remained for one hundred years until fourteen-year-old Mozart heard it once and transcribed the work in full, from memory, and sent it out into the world.

The top C in the *Miserere* is considered one of the most exceptional moments in musical history, like the musical equivalent of The Great Pyramid of Giza. The solo voice of a boy soprano climbs out of the chorus to sing the most heart-rending musical phrase, with the purest high C. The chorus resumes, the voice momentarily anchored within it, only to once more break free and soar. And we, the listeners, sense that an exquisite insight into the purpose of our existence is just out of reach, creating a tension that is hard to bear.

Music's magic

When music meets theatre, something magical happens. Most of us don't sing our way through life's dramas and crises, but in musicals and opera – *Hamilton*, *The Lion King*, *The Marriage of Figaro* – the music intensifies the pathos of tragedy, inflates comedy and magnifies joy and happiness. When the show ends, we carry away with us both the story and the song.

During lockdown, musicals helped to carry us through. In living rooms around the world re-enactments of iconic scenes from musicals were created and shared with strangers online, joining us together in a cultural touchpoint of laughter and song.

Emotional effects

The musical *Come from Away* is set in a small Newfoundland town at the time when thirty-eight international flights were diverted to Gander Airport following the terrorist attacks on the World Trade Centre. It is a story of welcome, generosity and hope in the shadow of the 9/11 catastrophe. The story is about place and people and an unparalleled moment in time, but it's the music that connects us so intimately with the characters. The rhythms guide us through the emotional landscape. The music dips and we follow it down, it soars and takes our heart with it.

This is just one example amongst thousands where music's power fills needs in us that we might otherwise have thought only travel can serve.

In ballet and dance, the human body enacts the music in all of its emotional timbres, creating the most eloquent form of expression. To watch ballet is to truly get lost in the moment. The ballet of *Romeo and Juliet* takes Shakespeare's play and amplifies the emotional rollercoaster with Prokofiev's glorious music and exquisite choreography. It's a great introduction to ballet, and the music that accompanies the fight between the Montagues and Capulets has won over many a rock music diehard.

We know music is meaningful when we reflect on how it opens sporting events around the world, whether it's the first organ notes that energise the Boston Red Sox crowd, or the thumping opening chords of *We Are The Champions* at an ice hockey game, or the anthem-like singing of *You'll Never Walk Alone* at the start of every Liverpool football match (while the Leeds' supporters compete with their rendition of *Marching on Together*). It's there to celebrate the occasion, intensify the atmosphere, build anticipation and unite the crowd.

Myths and music

Nitmiluk (Katherine) Gorge, in Australia's Northern Territory, is an ancient land with deep spiritual significance to the Jawoyn people. A place of songlines and ceremony and rock art, of high sandstone cliffs, waterholes and waterfalls and spectacular sunsets.

Some years ago it was the location for a performance of Carl Orff's *Carmina Burana*. Here was the world's oldest continuous culture playing host to German medieval poetry set to 19th century music.

Imagine the slow pacing drums and the rising voices of the chorus echoing through the Gorge. Such settings take music – and us – somewhere else completely.

A personalised playlist

When we look for meaning in life, music offers one powerful answer. It fulfils and fortifies in so many ways. Bach's *Goldberg Variations* have accompanied me through my years of study, playing in the background, keeping me sane and focussed. Hospitals use music to reduce the need for medication, to speed healing and calm children before surgery. Stroke victims who have lost their ability to speak are taught to express their needs in song.

It's always there for us, whatever our need. We can create a soundtrack to take us to places within ourselves, adding depth and pleasure and building resilience. With the push of a button we can summon music to reflect our mood, improve our day, enhance an occasion.

We can fill our diary with the places we will see on our world tour. Or we can create a rewarding staycation by filling it with the music we want to explore. A Greek music festival or a Russian ballet performance. New Orleans jazz in some grungy basement, or Cuban rumba. Irish jigs played in pubs, Berlin-style nightclub shows, Estonian choirs in church halls and oud players in cafés.

We take something from each – a mosaic tile of sound – and fit all the vibrant colours and surprising shapes together to create our own personalised soundtrack to guide us through a more cosmopolitan and fulfilling life.

It's always there for us, whatever our need. We can create a soundtrack to take us to places within ourselves, adding depth and pleasure and building resilience. With the push of a button we can summon music to reflect our mood, improve our day, enhance an occasion.

Getting lost in art

*'The aim of art is to represent not the outward appearance of
things, but their inward significance.'*

Aristotle

Be open to challenge

It's not only travel that lets us see the world from different angles. Art offers
a whole host of panoramas to shift our many perspectives, to encourage us
to think anew.

It can act on our emotions, making us feel sad, bewildered or uplifted. It
can interrogate and subvert conventional thinking, upsetting what we have
always taken for granted. It can be avant-garde, foretelling what lies in store
for us. It can say what is not easily put into words. It asks that we approach
it not only with an expectation of pleasure, but with an open mind and
preparedness to be led somewhere challenging.

There's art everywhere we look. We find paintings in churches and
sculpture in parks. Grand historical homes are over-full with artworks,
including furniture. There's splendid architecture in city centres and country
towns. There's a move for stunningly designed private residences to open as
house museums for public viewing. There's street art; there's wildly creative
playground equipment and gloriously designed gardens. In my local town,
First Nations art of local fauna is embedded in the pavements.

Good, bad, beautiful?

Art historian Nancy Langham-Hooper likes to use the example of Aunt Bertha's painting to demonstrate that our personal reaction to an artwork is all that matters. 'You might love Aunt Bertha's landscape paintings,' Nancy said to me. 'You may recognise she wasn't much of an artist, but her paintings remind you of her kindness and vivacity. They remind you of sun-drenched afternoons in her garden, bees active amongst the hollyhocks, magpies splashing in the birdbath, lemonade with clinking ice cubes. For all these reasons they are important to you. So, is her art good or bad? Who cares?'

Art moves us when it touches us personally. Aunt Bertha's paintings have merit of their own. There's nothing to be gained by comparing them with Constable's famous landscapes. Of course, some artworks are elevated above others, in recognition of an exceptional interpretation of the human spirit or of nature. Even if we don't understand how it is achieved, we can acknowledge that the master artists delve more deeply. Which doesn't take us much further forward on the question about how to judge art, except to encourage us to learn more.

Labyrinths of surprise

Travel bloggers are forever promoting the merits of getting lost in foreign places as the one sure way to chance upon unexpected surprises and catch hidden glimpses of ourselves. Yet in a city near home, there's a very special place where getting lost really will reap boundless rewards.

Art museums and galleries. Only exhibiting works of art, these surprise-laden labyrinths encourage us to lose our bearings, on purpose and intelligently. We turn a corner to be met with beauty, intrigue, strangeness, humour or inspiration. Another corner and we stumble upon a work that sparks uncanny self-recognition. In such ways, these galleries bring the exotic and strange home to us while simultaneously expanding our sense of self.

Over the past couple of decades there's been a revolution in the way galleries present art. There is now a spirit of egalitarianism that art is for everyone, speaks to everyone, and has the capacity to enrich all lives.

The big public art museums have become welcoming, liberal and non-judgemental places for social gathering as much as for visual feasting; for entertainment as much as for edification. They display works of art found both in and outside the mould of the traditional artist. There's as likely to be an immersive exhibition of soundscapes as of old-masters' oil paintings. There are no set rules of what and how to view art. We can take account of what the critics say about a particular artwork, and we can read the curators' notes, but ultimately it comes down to how we personally respond to it.

The world of art is vast. A museum might borrow artworks from institutions around the country to explore aspects of national identity. Or from a number of other countries for a retrospective exhibition of a single artist's work, or to survey a specific art movement. Weeks of globetrotting could never achieve the same breadth of exploration and comparison. And while we can travel to Amsterdam to see Van Gogh's *Sunflowers*, if we wait, there's a chance it will come to an art museum near home.

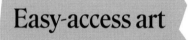

Easy-access art

A regional town may have a fantastic smaller-scale art museum which focuses on art from their corner of the world. Commercial galleries will often showcase local and lesser-known artists and host events, usually for free. Just because the art is for sale doesn't mean we can't view and appreciate it. At a fair or flea market, we may find the next Andy Warhol at a bargain price.

Many small towns have thriving artist communities, their art appearing in a range of places: public buildings, cafés and shopping malls as well as local art galleries. Town festivals, markets, country fairs and the local Rotary Club, often run by volunteers, fill another role in supporting local artists. They encourage anyone to have a go. It's about wellbeing and belonging, putting locals first to promote a more fulfilling life for both artists and those who come to see the art.

We *look* at Niagara Falls, but we try
to *see* into the soul of Rembrandt in
one of his self-portraits.

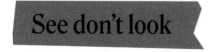

See don't look

Curators of art exhibitons have a saying: *To see is to think*. It's a concept
that goes to the heart of finding meaning in life. We strive to disrupt our
complacency, expand our horizons and search for hints to answer those
why and *how* questions.

Seeing is different from *looking*. Looking is noticing the obvious. In a
painting, that might be the materials used, the composition, colours and
symbolism. *Seeing* is a deeper engagement where we reflect on what is in
front of us, what it tells us, how it affects us. We *look* at Niagara Falls, but
we try to *see* into the soul of Rembrandt in one of his self-portraits.

We need context to see. Context adds depth and colour to understanding.
We might start by reading about the artist's life and the history of the time;
explore why the work was created and what it meant to the artist. Fortunately,
curators now aid us in our endeavours as they include contextual information
to answer these very questions to help and encourage us to see. We need to
give art time to stir us, to awaken a new understanding.

We need to give art
time to stir us,
to awaken a
new understanding.

Give art a chance

Jackson Pollock's painting *Blue Poles* caused an uproar in Australia when it was purchased with public money for the National Gallery of Australia in 1973. The public didn't understand it; it was way too abstract. It did, though, spark a national conversation about art!

When American Pollock painted *Blue Poles* in 1952, he was already at the height of his career but depressed in the aftermath of World War II. He and his friend Tony Smith were both drunk when they started the work. They threw paint randomly onto a canvas lying on the floor. There's a bare footprint and small shards from smashed wine glasses imbedded in the work. And there are eight sort-of blue poles leaning at odd angles. The result of chaos.

Such context helps to explain how and why Pollock chose to communicate both internal and external psychological and social upheaval through abstract expressionism.

What art will emerge from the pandemic? How will artists interpret the altered times we are stepping into? How might we reinterpret and find new relevance in existing art?

While our travel opportunities remain constrained, we can use our holiday time to undertake journeys into art to hone our ability to see what is being hinted at, emphasised and symbolised. How? Why? And if we return to travel, we will find that our explorations through art have equipped us with a priceless skill of not just looking, but of seeing to understand.

The real thing

Has Instagram stopped us from seeing art? We've all seen the selfies. People standing with their backs to the *Mona Lisa*, using the famous painting as a mere backdrop to their I-was-here moment. Presented with a once-in-a-lifetime opportunity to see the original masterpiece, why do so many people waste it by *looking* at it only through their smartphone?

Art requires our undivided attention. When we stand and absorb the real thing, we *see* the effect of Da Vinci's use of sfumato (the hazy, soft-focus effect that blends light, shade and colour without borders). We ask ourselves, what makes Mona Lisa's gaze so enchanting, her smile so enigmatic? How is it that she appears both ethereal and tangibly real? (We can buy a good-quality reproduction in the gift shop later.) When our view is not mitigated through a lens, we will take away more in our heads and hearts than can ever be captured in a snap.

Hidden treasures

We might first be lured into a large public art museum by a blockbuster, the chance to see works by the big names. There's nothing wrong with that, of course, except that there's the tendency to think, having paid our money, we must see everything. So we dash from one work to the next giving them all the same amount of attention or inattention. We leave with a sensation similar to what we might feel after visiting a chocolate factory. Having over-indulged, we can't recall the difference between coconut rough and rocky road.

Blockbusters expose us to some of the best art in the world, making them crowd-drawing affairs. We shuffle along with the throng, peer over shoulders and around smartphones to get a glimpse of the masterpieces. Rarely is there the opportunity to stand quietly in front of a work we find interesting.

Keep in mind that a museum's permanent collection will be crowd-free yet full of gems. Art historian, Nancy Langham-Hooper, recommends that instead of one fatiguing binge-session in a gallery we turn our visits into mini adventures. 'Go little, go often,' she urges. Our regular visits reveal that not all of the art in museums is superlative. We learn to decide what qualifies as a masterpiece *for us*. Roaming through the labyrinth of artworks one day we may stumble on a seemingly insignificant work which becomes our favourite. We make it a friend, visit it often, get to know it intimately. We learn about its creator and the context of its creation. We give it time to do the talking and gradually work out where our love springs from.

While it might not be the head-over-heels tumult of falling for a fellow human, there's the same wonder and thrill. The same acknowledgement that our life has been made richer.

Falling for an angel

Antony Gormley's *Angel of the North* sculpture worked its way into my heart the first time I saw it, standing so erect and proud on a mound by the A1 road near Gateshead in north-east England. Perhaps it's the scale of the work (20m high with a wingspan of 54m) or that the wings tilt forward to give, as Gormley says, 'a sense of embrace'. Or perhaps it's the stunning simplicity, or the history of the site, where coalminers laboured beneath that mound for 200 years. Or perhaps it is because, standing beneath it, there's something transformative in the silence and stillness that the *Angel* evokes. Mostly, for me, the *Angel* is a meditation on what it means to be human.

There's a human-size version of the *Angel of the North* in the grounds of the National Gallery of Australia in Canberra – much easier for me to visit regularly. It's a more intimate *Angel*, this one, at peace amongst the gum trees with a backdrop of Lake Burley Griffin. 'Good morning, Angel', is my private ritual, a way of connecting with the sculpture and making it a little bit mine.

Expeditions through time and space

'A people without knowledge of their past history, origin and culture is like a tree without roots.'

Marcus Garvey

A journey like no other

On the forecourt of a city museum, I watch a gaggle of little kids in bright blue school uniforms, bubbling with anticipation. Their excitement is justified. They are about to embark on a journey like no other, one that will reveal to them the extraordinary scope of their world. They'll see all manner of creatures, from the tiniest insects to mammoth dinosaurs. They'll learn about the enormity of the universe, the diversity of the planet, the traditions and customs of their own community. They'll delve into the past and glimpse the future.

Gone are the days when they would have been led through dimly lit rooms full of dull and dusty collections. No talking! Do not touch! Now there's chatter and play, poking and prodding. Everything is presented in such a way that, young as they may be, they will get a sense of how they fit into the world.

I follow the children through the big glass doors inside, knowing that museums are as much for adults as for kids. We, too, can discover our place in the world through the vast array of travel-like stories about multiple destinations. We can pick and choose where we go and what we see. There's no crowded itinerary, we're free to explore in our own way and at our own pace. We can take our new insights home, where we have time to ruminate on what we have seen and learnt. We're free to revisit at any time.

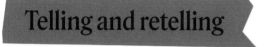

Collections that illustrate remarkable achievements of the past can be illuminating. They can also be the result of colonial plundering.

Telling and retelling

Museums originated in ancient Greece when collectors filled their mouseions with items that they believed would please the Muses, the goddesses of the arts. The Romans translated mouseion into the Latin word museum and continued the practice.

The first public museum opened in 1671, in Basel, Switzerland. It was followed by the Ashmolean Museum, Oxford, in 1683 then the British Museum in 1735, which the British Parliament directed should be aimed at universality. Likewise, the Smithsonian was established in 1846 for the increase and diffusion of knowledge.

These old, venerable institutions contain vast collections from around the world, showcasing important artifacts, collected over hundreds of years. They tell multiple stories, good and bad. Collections that illustrate remarkable achievements of the past can be illuminating. They can also be the result of colonial plundering.

Some of the world's most prestigious museums hold in their collections the cultural heritage of other countries – items stolen during empire expansion and colonisation, through war and duplicity. The impact of such losses continues to resonate down the generations of those who were the victims. Many museums now acknowledge historical wrongs by ethically reviewing and decolonising their collections and returning stolen items to their rightful owners.

As visitors to museums, we should be alert to the morality or otherwise of what we are viewing. We can learn to appreciate the stark difference between a collection that invites a deep understanding of other ways of life and one that perpetuates past wrongs.

A museum chrysalis

The Butterfly Conservatory at the American Museum of Natural History shows how far museums have advanced since the days of dusty cases of dead insects. In this lush, tropical enclosure, the approximately 500 butterfly specimens are alive, flying and resting. Catepillars munch on leaves, chrysalis dangle from branches.

Here we learn about the butterfly life cycle, the environments in which butterflies live, their role in the web of life and the dangers that threaten the survival of these stunning and essential creatures.

Choose a topic

Today, museums focus on what visitors want rather than reflecting the interests of their curators. We can choose a museum or an exhibition as we would choose a travel destination, to answer many of the questions we take with us on our travels. The Haitian Heritage Museum in Miami showcases Haitian culture, helping its visitors to understand the Caribbean nation without the need to book a flight or cruise. It also provides a continuing link between the diaspora and their roots, and celebrates the Haitian contribution to Florida's vitality.

So many varied topics are made available to us. Reality, for example. In cities around the world, Museums of Illusions use holograms, vortex tunnels, optical illusions, bottomless pits and rotated rooms to challenge our assumptions about reality. On one level, these museums are entertainment, tricking our brains and eyes in fun and creative ways. On another, they are serious educators, teaching us about vision, perception, the brain and science. They encourage us to explore beyond what we think we see. They bring us face to face with an age-old philosophical conundrum: is the world we perceive just an illusion?

The globally crowd-funded project Museum of Broken Relationships displays stories of love and loss. Los Angeles and Zagreb host permanent collections, and a touring exhibition has taken these universal stories to fifty other cities around the world.

Ellis Island Immigration Museum documents the arrival of twelve million immigrants into the USA over a sixty-two-year period. It is a symbol of the freedom and hope that accompanied the immigrants and a celebration of their enormous contribution to American society.

Planetariums, found in many cities, are museums of the night sky in all its wondrous splendour. They take us on a truly out-of-this-world expedition to stars and planets, meteors and satellites, mythologies and space stations.

The natural history collections of museums tell a multitude of stories, curated in a multitude of ways. Indeed, museums constitute the single largest source of information about the earth's biological diversity.

At the Library of Water in remote Iceland, twenty-four glass columns contain samples from jÖkulls – the Icelandic glaciers that are slowly melting as the planet heats. The library is a museum of ice in its melted form and a record of the damage we are inflicting.

The museums on our home turf provide us with something we will never find in a foreign-country museum – a personal connection.

I'm fascinated by museum exhibitions of the recent past that offer walks down memory lane. 'Oh, we had a toaster like that one'. 'A black bakelite dial telephone, just like Grandma's'. 'That poster of the *Desiderata* poem was on my bedroom wall all through my teenage years'. And, 'listen, they're playing *Lucy in the Sky with Diamonds*. I remember that song playing when I was growing up'. It feels like a confirmation that my own history is worth celebrating, that it has *significance*.

The museums on our home turf provide us with something we will never find in a foreign-country museum – a personal connection. They reflect what is important locally. They help us to puzzle out our own history, customs and environment, and therefore our own identity. They are keepers of our cultural memory.

National Trusts

The world watched in horror as Notre Dame burned. A global mourning began for what was being lost. Astonishing beauty, gothic architecture, religious tradition, a trove of stories, a vital part of French identity. A world treasure, inherited from the past, loved in the present, and expected to last forever. Our heartache – a consequence of loss far beyond bricks and mortar – reinforced the need to preserve places that encapsulate history and culture.

National Trusts the world over understand that to preserve the built, natural and cultural heritage ensures the past isn't erased. They safeguard heritage buildings, monuments and landscapes as stores of our cultural, social, economic and political histories. All provide a record of where we have come from and who we are, they help guide a course for the future.

Their charter of protection translates into a sense of continuity and stability, identity and belonging. Heritage, tangible and intangible, is our rock in the defence against these times of rapid change and our commemoration of distinctiveness in a rapidly homogenising world. It is our guard against the fraudulent rewriting of history. Our support of organisations such as National Trusts, either through donation, volunteering or membership, helps to protect our heritage.

Be inspired and rewarded

Our imagination is provoked by unfamiliar sights and experiences. It's what we ask of travel but museums do provoke the same. Better than travel, museums are local, generate far fewer emissions, and offer lots of contextual detail. Unlike so much of commercialised travel, they strive for authenticity.

They inspire and motivate us towards greater knowledge and more critical thinking. They invite curiosity and endlessly reward us with ever-expanding insights into culture, history, science and the natural world. They demonstrate how intimately we are a part of our species, our planet, and the universe.

Without going far, we can discover distant lands and distant times. We can seek out the exotic, unusual and downright weird. We can delve into the tapestries of Tudor England, or contemplate an early Buddhist bronze. The American Museum of Natural History took us on a trek through the human cranium in its Brain exhibition. At the Museum of Old and New Art (MONA) in Hobart, Tasmania, we can watch (somewhat squeamishly) as the *Cloaca* performs the work of the digestive tract.

How stories are told

Museum curators artfully reconstruct the past in the present through a combination of artifacts and information. They blend disciplines such as history, biology, cosmology and philosophy to explain these stories.

They reveal the skills of previous generations that have brought us to this point in time. They remind us that in many ways we are not superior to everyone who has gone before us. In some cases, they display items that make our current skills look puny. At the Lofotr Viking Museum in Norway archaeologists continue to puzzle over how 10th century Vikings produced such strong, flexible swords. The marble sculptures at the Acropolis Museum in Athens are of unrivalled artistic excellence – and they were created in the period 480–79 BCE.

A clever curation can bring a collection of objects together to explore expansive topics. In *A History of the World in a Hundred Objects* Neil McGregor, Director of the British Museum, took us globetrotting across a vast landscape of human endeavour spanning 2250 years. The exhibition told the story of civilisation through objects from Egyptian mummies to Easter Island statues, from gold coins to a solar-charged lamp.

McGregor said that the aim of the project was to examine how humans have shaped the world and how the world has shaped us. Objects grand and humble were selected for what they told about people and places – not just history's big stories, but those of their everyday lives. The objects speak for those silenced by time and illiteracy. Along the way, McGregor reminded us that stone objects (with a few rare exceptions) are all that remain of ninety-five per cent of human existence.

The Cyrus Cylinder

One of the rarest objects in the British Museum, the Cyrus Cylinder was created 2600 years ago in Persia. This baked-clay cylinder is completely covered in Babylonian writing. It is Cyrus the Great's declaration that he intended to govern by consent rather than by fear.

Referred to as the first bill of human rights, and compared to the Magna Carta, it is the earliest expression of how a society composed of different ethnicities, religions, habits and languages might be held together. Cyrus promised his people rest from their exhaustion and servitude, the right to worship their choice of god, and freedom to return home (in particular the Jewish slaves to Jerusalem). The symbolism of the Cyrus Cylinder – tolerance and freedom – is as relevant today as it was in the early years of civilisation. Such an invaluable message, contained in an ancient object, preserved in a museum.

Curation on the run

During the period of self-isolation, many museums sent out calls for stories, photos, videos, posters, signage. Anything that recorded how ordinary people were coping with the life-altering experience of lockdown. This was a rare shift in the nature of curation: collecting in real time, documenting as history unfolded, preserving the present for future exhibitions that will provide a snapshot of an unprecedented event.

That's the thing about museums, they're for everyone – at every level and every interest.

Go for the fun

While many collections can be viewed online there's nothing like actually being there. It's not all seriousness and hard work, of course. Museums can be entertaining, fun and social. They are communal, inclusive places – and that might be all we want from them. Or we might seek knowledge, from a brief moment of enlightenment to a deeper absorption in detail. We might go for the guided tours or the annual blockbuster, the café or the gift shop. That's the thing about museums, they're for everyone – at every level and every interest.

The world of books

*'Had I the power, I would scatter libraries over the whole land,
as the sower sows his wheat field.'*

Horace Mann

More than books

Libraries are synonymous with books, but they offer far more. They venture into exhibitions, internet access, magazines and newspapers, lectures and learning programmes. They are custodians of heritage, through archives, artworks and artifacts that speak to the history of their place. When we enter these sanctums of books, we submerge ourselves in the hushed atmosphere, to soak up the very essence of civilisation.

Libraries are nurturers of wisdom. They give us the opportunity to take in as much information as we are able, at our own pace, across as many topics as we please – an incremental layering of knowledge that makes us better navigators through life.

A library can be a refuge. A warm, secure place for the homeless, a community for the lonely, free reading and internet access for the poor. A quiet space for those in overcrowded housing, a place to meet friends, to study, or to read a newspaper in peace. As places of genuine social inclusion, libraries are outstanding and essential.

Between the covers of thousands of volumes lie every place we could ever wish to visit – across space and through time. When we decide to holiday at home, we can spend the days of our staycation poring over an atlas, consulting an encyclopedia, browsing through histories. This might not be true travel but it reminds me of how French peasants enjoyed truffles by proxy. The truffles, being too valuable for them to keep for their own consumption, were put into a basket with fresh eggs overnight to allow the eggs to absorb the strong musky flavour. Truffle-infused scramble eggs are, in their own right, a culinary delight.

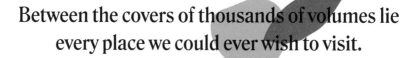

Between the covers of thousands of volumes lie every place we could ever wish to visit.

Trailblazing through the stacks

In cities around the world, large public libraries – old and new – are often magnificent buildings of gravitas and glory. They celebrate what they house, the essence and history of humanity. Their grandeur is a direct reflection of their central importance as cultural institutions.

So many of them – in so many places – are worth visiting as destinations in their own right. What they offer and the way in which they are cared for tells us something fundamental about local social values. There's an important difference though between the way we visit libraries as tourists and the way we visit our home libraries. With one, it is to see, with the other, it is to use.

Be illuminated

Despite their age, the 1300-year-old Lindisfarne Gospels have lost none of their power to awe. Their illuminated pages of gold and brilliant colours and of elaborate artwork continue to astound those who gaze upon them.

We can see them at the British Library, but we can also explore them online. Not just the Lindisfarne Gospels, but hundreds of medieval texts. We can skip from the National Library of Bulgaria to the Bibliotheques de Reims, across to Biblioteca de Catalunya and on to Abbey Library of St.Gall – all before lunchtime. The British Library and Bibliothèque nationale de France have together made eight hundred illuminated medieval manuscripts available online as a virtual public asset. Browsing the site our senses are not only stirred by the splendour of the artifacts but by the tales they tell of ordinary life, religion, the law and the music of the times.

Libraries are leading adopters of technology, digitalising their holdings from these historical gems to the latest ebooks. Illumination comes in many forms.

Go local

Local libraries are as much community hubs as places to borrow books. While the big libraries are open-hearted, trustworthy places, we connect most intimately at the local level. Exploration and discovery are warmly encouraged and no-one is going to judge us, intimidate us, question our right to enter, look over our shoulder or demand a fee. Librarians don't even shush us these days!

Ask almost any writer where their love of words began and they are most likely to extol the virtues of their childhood libraries. They'll recall their wide-eyed astonishment at so much choice, of lugging home bags of books, of agonising over which to read first. They'll praise the librarians who never spoke down to them, and encouraged them to read, read, read. Without local libraries, so many writers would never have picked up a pen, so many great books would never have come into being.

At my local library, in addition to the books, magazines, newspapers, computers, movies and music, there's tea and coffee, comfortable furniture and spotless toilets. Looking around, there are people of all ages and walks of life. An elderly man is getting help to complete an online form. Little kids have come for Rhyme-time. Researchers are at work in the local-history room. Teenagers are scanning the shelves for anything from science textbooks to teen drama. A man in hi-vis jacket is applying for a job online. A young woman is asking a librarian what she should read next. There are two women knitting and quietly chatting. The man who drives the mobile library bus is choosing books on behalf of his remote rural readers. This is the wonderful, eclectic mix of a modern community library.

As the motto goes, Libraries Change Lives – for the better. We need to defend them against the threat of their demise through economic rationalism. Public libraries, large and small, have high socio-economic value (even in hardcore return-on-investment terms). A community is significantly diminished when its library closes.

Library funding is often linked to library visits, so our patronage is library protection. Holidays at home are the perfect opportunity to start becoming a regular user. Just ask the librarian how to join.

Libraries at home

Sometimes (in my case, often) we don't just want to borrow books. We want to own them. We want them on our shelves to revisit like old friends. We treat them with affectionate intimacy.

To build up a library over time is to mark the passage of the years in a very personal way. We lift a book from the shelf, weigh it in our hands and remember what was happening in our lives the last time we opened it. It has a place in our life's story.

In *Hamlet*, Polonius counsels his son to neither a borrower nor a lender be. It's not something I subscribe to when it comes to books. There's such joy in lending what we've loved to the people who matter in our life and in reading the books they have enjoyed. When we lend a book, we reveal a little of ourselves. The recommendation is a disclosure of what we believe is important, in life beyond the book, and who amongst our friends shares our sentiments. Reading the same books becomes a bedrock of our relationship, a cornerstone of our conversations.

Join a book club

The beauty of book clubs is that they get us reading, although that's only one reason to join. We meet new people with a similar interest (reading) but with widely varying tastes and interpretations.

We're persuaded to read books we might otherwise ignore – not always a good thing, but we're saved from becoming too narrow in our reading habits. We tackle books that demand debate, such as Lionel Shriver's *We Need to Talk about Kevin*, Colson Whitehead's *The Underground Railway*, or Christos Tsiolkas's *The Slap* – troubling stories that we need to discuss with others to unravel and ease our discomfort.

As a group, we use a book as a springboard into discussions around emotional and moral complexities, and listen to other points of view. All the while we are expanding our horizons beyond the book's covers.

And then there's the coffee and cake afterwards.

How to join? Ask at your local bookshop or library, find virtual groups online, ask amongst friends.

How to choose

Bibliophilia is a love of books, a *bibliophile* being the lover. *Bibliomania* refers to a mania for collecting and possessing them. Fortunately, there is a very pleasant and convenient cure for *bibliomania*.

Outside on the street, all is bustle and noise. We step through the door of our favourite bookshop, into sanctuary – a calming atmosphere that invites leisurely browsing. It's a civilised space, no blaring musak, pushing crowds, or raucous announcements. There's the scent of fresh print and paper (*bibliosmia!*). Customers unconsciously lower their voices. Reverence? Perhaps so, because this is where booklovers are in their element. It's their church. And like a church, it's both a public and a deeply private space. It's a place of commerce, certainly, but also quite palpably, a place of creativity, entertainment, knowledge and art.

There are tables piled with the latest releases, there are obscure classics and sumptuous cookery books. There are thrillers and prize-winners, history books and travel guides. There are steamy romances and celebrity biographies. Head on one side, we scan the shelves and read the titles running down the spines. When we come across an author we know it's like finding a familiar face in a crowd.

Life is short and books are many.

Life is short and books are many. Choosing something suitable from the vast range can be daunting. Fortunately, the mark of a good bookshop is its helpful and knowledgeable staff, only too keen to guide us. They'll tailor their recommendations to our interests; they'll make it personal. We might think of them as matchmakers.

Bookshops are about more than just selling books. They are part of the neighbourhood, the community, the family. They support local writers who would otherwise struggle to be read. They hold book readings, launches, a whole range of literary events. They are places where we can fall into exuberant conversation about the latest bestseller with a total stranger.

Bookshops let us browse. They allow us to indulge in the pleasure of holding a book in our hands and skimming through pages. They make possible stumbling upon something interesting that an algorithm would never pick for us, or that we'd never find in the overwhelming lists of the big online retailers.

Showrooming – the act of browsing in a bookshop (any shop, in fact), even asking for advice then buying online – risks the loss of everything that bookshops offer.

Bookshops are about more than just selling books. They are part of the neighbourhood, the community, the family.

Celebrate the written word

Writers' festivals bring together authors, poets, journalists, dramatists, historians, scientists, politicians and academics. Celebrity, established, emerging or undiscovered. These festivals showcase all the varied approaches to the art: controversial, inventive, intriguing, informative, funny and entertaining. There are writers' festivals the world over and they come in all sizes, from world-renowned events such as the Berlin International Literature Festival and Bangladesh's Dhaka Lit Fest, to smaller, regional affairs, to those held in local libraries and bookshops. Like a world tour, we move from one speaker to the next and discover something new and enlightening in each talk. We travel with these writers to destinations we might never have the opportunity to visit. We learn about perspectives of life in those places that, even if we did visit, we would never witness nor begin to comprehend.

Writers, booksellers, librarians – they are our true and trusted travel guides. They help to keep us free from the affliction *abibliophobia*, the fear of not having a book waiting to be read after finishing the one we're reading. As George R.R. Martin declared, 'A reader lives a thousand lives before he dies. The man who never reads lives only one'.

Home advantage

*'Friendship improves happiness and abates misery by
doubling our joys and dividing our grief.'*

Marcus Tullius Cicero

An antidote for loneliness

Travel is often motivated by the expectation of meeting new people. We've
seen our friend's Instagram photo, standing before an amazing backdrop,
arm slung around the shoulders of a new-found soulmate. It conveys the
message that making new friends on the road is easy.

In the next city, it's another view, another soulmate. Our friend seems to
be having so much fun. Their photos persuade us to book a holiday so that we,
too, can experience this carefree connection with new and fascinating people.

And then we come home ...

We know in our hearts that to build lasting friendships takes time, effort
and being in each other's company through good times and bad. Unlike trips
away, we are at home for the long run – this communal place where we can
form the bonds that will carry us into the future.

Togetherness comes in so many varieties, congregations, charity
organisations, social clubs, sports teams. All formed around common
interests. While such organisations have their particular purpose, their
overarching value is providing an environment in which people can be
social and supportive of each other. Being with others, giving and receiving
companionship and care, is a way of living with purpose.

It need not be complicated or daunting and it need not stretch the budget. For a small membership fee we can join the local chess or photography club. For nothing at all we can volunteer at our chosen charity. With a pair of goggles, we can sign up to a swimming squad. With a racket in hand, we can join a badminton club. We get together each and every week, building relationships, cherishing togetherness, overcoming loneliness.

We're a species that needs companionship. A search for genuine, enduring ways to connect with like-minded people is part of our quest for meaning in life. Sport is an interest that answers this.

Good sport

Sport is play with rules that mirror our embedded values. To believe in the game, the rules have to be fair and appropriate. We respect them for the good of the game and those who flout them are punished. There's no 'I' in team, we work together and the whole becomes greater than the parts. We acknowledge those who excel in their field and shame those who cheat. We ritualise the game as if it were a religion. The best players become our heroes and role models.

Sport is graceful. There's an elegance in the way our bodies move in sport. We reach impossibly wide to hit a tennis ball, or leap skywards to shoot a ball through a hoop, or slice through the water one powerful stroke after another. Rhythm, strength, nuance, freedom, balance – we could be ballet dancing.

There's rhythm in teamwork too, in becoming familiar with how the minds and bodies of our fellow players work, adjusting to fit into the play, and striving to perform at our peak for each other. We learn to plan our actions and take lessons from past mistakes, using our minds as much as our bodies.

Sport is purpose. It gives us a reason to belong, a common language, a shared activity. We learn to win and lose with grace. It is an integral part of life balance, countering work with play.

Sport is one of the few pursuits in life that we begin in childhood and easily carry into adulthood and older age. We might start with junior athletics, move on to tennis or indoor soccer, then to lawn bowls. That's the amazing thing about the range of sports available, there's a game and a level to suit everyone.

Sport is purpose.
It gives us a reason
to belong, a common
language, a shared
activity. We learn to win
and lose with grace.

Sport for everyone

Some sports have no barriers to age. At my local yacht club, the sailors range in age from eight to eighty. The juniors begin in dinghies, looking like ducklings out on the water. The hotshot adults sail fast and demanding Olympic-class keelboats. With the passing years, skippers and crew migrate to the more sedate pace of cruising yachts.

Some sailors seek an afternoon's onboard companionship that just happens to coincide with a yacht race while others are highly competitive. Some are pretty ordinary sailors while others compete in state, national and international regattas. Regardless, in the clubhouse after the race, the mood is buoyant, as conditions and tactics are dissected over hot food and cold beer. The sport has united and uplifted, regardless of vessel, age, gender or financial status.

Sport is universal. We find it in all cultures, and nations wear their national sport like a badge of honour. Politicians love to bathe in its glory. Schools recognise it as integral to the curriculum, for health and lessons in life skills. It fills newspapers – the same game over and over, and always different. Ex-pats introduce their homeland sport and their adopted country embraces the novelty.

It's a great leveller. In any country, it only takes one group of kids to bring out a soccer ball and other kids are joining in the game in no time – no shared language needed!

The game mirrors the topsy-turvy nature of our lives and gives us an outlet to express raw emotion through the highs and lows of the match. In this way, sport is our recreation: how we re-create ourselves, sloughing off the pressures of everyday life by immersing ourselves in an alternative existence.

A common cause

Powerfully and universally, sport influences and shapes who we are and what we value. It unites us – players and spectators alike – through common cause and gives us a reason to celebrate.

It connects us across communities and across the globe. Linked through our televisions and devices we are part of the game without leaving home. We understand that we can remain in our separate corners of the globe and still be one big audience. When we watch Wimbledon, the PGA Cup, the Tour de France and the Monaco Grand Prix separately in our homes, the event takes us out into the world and brings the world home to us.

United through sport

There are moments in sporting history when the world comes together and shows its better self – when we recognise what binds us.

In Sydney, on 19 September 2000, Eric Moussambani Malonga prepared to compete in the first heat of the 100m freestyle. A wildcard draw allowed him to represent Equatorial Guinea at the Olympic Games. He had been swimming for eight months, training alone in the 12m pool of the Hotel Malabo. His first sight of the Sydney Olympics's 50m pool filled him with dread; the prowess of the other swimmers was terrifying.

The other two swimmers broke before the gun and were disqualified, leaving Moussambani to swim alone. He almost didn't finish but he could hear the crowd cheering him on and he struggled to the end. He recorded the slowest time in Olympic history.

He feared ridicule. Instead, for that magical, poignant moment 17,000 spectators, the media and the world's TV audience united in their celebration for this one man. They travelled the length of the pool and back with Moussambani, not as various nationalities but as one massive cheer squad.

As the COVID-19 pandemic spread, one match after another was abandoned, events shut down, doors closed, tournaments were cancelled, and the Tokyo Olympic Games were postponed. There was a general air of mourning around the world. This was no trivial response. Losing the opportunity to watch these events brought home how much we care about sharing moments across oceans and cultures.

For many small communities, the loss of the weekend game during self-isolation was the unravelling of the threads that bound people together. Sport for many communities is a unifier, a release, something to live for, a way of coping, a cornerstone of mental and social health. It's the committee and the volunteers and the local businesses who provide sponsorship. It's the common topic of conversation that keeps people connected from one game to the next. Through its absence, local sport was never so clearly exposed as an essential component in community life.

Cheer from the sidelines

The atmosphere in the stands can be as thrilling as the play on the field or court or rink. There's the camaraderie of the roaring crowd when a goal is scored, the collective groan when a wicket falls, the combined gasp as the golf ball circles the hole, the held breath before a basketball sails through the basket. And when the runner slides into home base, or the player shoots the puck into the net, the tribe rises in one fluid motion, as if it were a single beast. These are intoxicating experiences, regardless of whether it's junior rugby, district hockey or the FA Cup.

The team's symbolism and rituals bind us: the storytelling, the colours, the mascots, the songs and the flags all contribute to identifying and uniting members. We share the language and know the history. We define ourselves by our loyalty and dedication. In the cap and scarf we wear, we show our team is part of who we are. Going to a game with friends and strangers builds a sense of community, even family. Who cares about the ethnicity or gender or age of the people around us? We're moved to laugh together, cry, throw our arms around each other. Behaviour out of place elsewhere is acceptable in the name of the game. For a few hours, the match is vitally important. Our own struggles and misfortunes are forgotten and, win or lose, we gain in the good fortune of being one of many.

Becoming a member of our favourite sports club knits us more tightly into the team and the action. Or we can go a step further. Being part of the behind-the-scenes crew brings rewards of group involvement, friendship and purpose. There's the game, the playing and the watching, and there's all the ancillary roles to make it happen. We might contribute existing skills or learn new ones. There is fundraising, recruitment, managing finances, feeding the team, writing grant applications, even helping with coach and team development.

The relationships we develop with teammates, fellow fans and co-volunteers have a special alchemy beyond the communal. There's trust and shared commitment and a deep sense of belonging. There's an alleviation of loneliness.

Home and away

There are benefits in being an armchair spectator. We see the ball up close, the highlights are rerun, and the commentary helps us to follow the action. We can watch any sport taking place anywhere in the world, as it happens, without the need to travel. At home, we can expand our interests in the sports of other nations. We can re-watch the Grand Final that our team won back in the 1960s.

But nothing beats being there, watching the players in real life, being caught up in the momentum, enthusiasm and excitement. There's pleasure in being outside, even if the weather is foul. Our team can hear us cheering them on. We come face to face with the opposition. On the tram after a major game, I've watched people wearing opposing team colours having a lively and friendly conversation about the goal that won the day.

Part three

The pleasures of being grounded

There's no place like it

*'I could be bounded in a nutshell and count myself
a king of infinite space'.*

Hamlet, William Shakespeare

A place to stay

In this final part of the book, we move inside. Not completely, there's still
plenty to do out in our neighbourhood, but there's also much joy to be found
in the physical space within which we live. A staycation gives us time to
embrace and re-connect with home – house, apartment, cabin or castle.
Exploring the elements of our culture is one way of finding meaning in life,
discovering what it means to be at home is another.

Re-evaluating home

Calamity, they say, is a great teacher. When COVID-19 struck, our lives
changed dramatically and irrevocably. All the plans that we had made
in great confidence slipped through our fingers like sand. Great blanks
appeared in our calendars. Our favourite gathering places closed. Suddenly
confined indoors, physical home was all we had.

For many people, being locked within four walls for months on end was
far from easy. Self-isolation meant the abandonment of the usual physical
social networks. It brought loneliness and boredom. The bricks and mortar

of home had been for many little more than an address, somewhere to sleep, wash socks, maybe heat up a tin of soup. Every interest was pursued out in the world in the company of friends. Those four walls were no substitute for the places that had always felt like home. In pubs, clubs and cafés, noise and crowds had been central to a sense of place and belonging.

But after a few weeks so many of us started to report an awakening, like a dawning friendship. As we settled into home's shapes and spaces, we renewed our relationship with objects we'd not noticed for years. We reshuffled our daily routines and found the new patterns a comfort. We listened, perhaps for the first time, to the birds and wind in the trees, and noticed the play of light on the ceiling. Many who had disregarded home before spoke of coming to appreciate it for the first time.

While we hankered for the outside world, we also learned the value of home as both a resource and a refuge. We learned to entertain ourselves in ways, weeks earlier, we would have scorned. Jigsaw puzzles? Sourdough breadmaking? You have to be kidding. We reassessed and relearned what matters most in life: each other, music, books, hobbies, games and daydreams. We came to know the people who lived in the apartment above and the house next door.

All the while we were learning, through our growing self-sufficiency, how to fortify our lives – for now and into the future.

We learned how to dwell. We discovered the seeds of contentment.

The call of home

At a street market in Agrigento, Sicily, an elderly woman wanted to sell me a Jew's harp, an ancient small instrument held in the mouth. She asked where I came from. 'Australia! Così lontano!' So far away, she moaned. Her words unsettled me, casting a net of homesickness over my day. She clutched my arm as she explained that the instrument's resonance conveyed yearning and sadness, feelings of displacement – the lament of the diaspora. This, she was sure, was how I must feel being so far from home. I bought the small harp. It plays happy, lively music as well as sad. But that elderly Sicilian had, nevertheless, touched a chord of yearning in my heart that returns whenever I'm far from home.

Where we belong

We are, at heart, more nest builders than nomads. Even as ardent travellers, we keep the idea of home close, a talisman worn against the skin to reassure us that no matter where we are, there is an anchor we can always return to. A magnet that inevitably draws us back.

But home is familiar and it's easy to confuse familiarity with mundanity. We rush off to find elsewhere what we fail to notice in the place where we belong.

We're dreaming

We stay in a charming village and in a holiday frame of mind, we delude ourselves that we could make it home. We sit at an outdoor café and watch the locals – their pace appears to be so delightfully unhurried, their lives endlessly fascinating. We let the morning drift as we dream about living here. This is somewhere we could live a new and better life.

Such dreams contribute to our holiday enjoyment. But they're only dreams, enticing because we see only the superficial, not the substratum where real life goes on. We forget what difficulties our cultural and language barriers would impose over time. All those baffling unwritten codes. We would need to find a reliable dentist, fathom local by-laws and master the banking system. Those long, relaxed brunches would morph into eating muesli, standing at the sink. And those locals who seem to live such perfect lives? They have mortgages, unsatisfying jobs, difficult teenagers, broken washing machines – all the accoutrements of real life just like us.

In foreign places, our hosts see us for what we are, tourists. Largely indistinguishable from one another, we are not part of their community, nor do they want us to be. From their perspective we are an important source of income but will-of-the-wisps – here today gone tomorrow – so there is no need to get to know us, no need to make an effort beyond what their role demands. Hospitality and courtesy are not the same as an invitation to belong.

To preserve their identity and ways of life, our hosts establish backstage regions for themselves, where they can go about their everyday lives hidden from inquisitive eyes. These are the places where home remains authentically itself rather than entertainment for tourists.

We also cultivate our own protective backstages – our physical home, along with our local library, bookshop, park, gym, market, or the café where we meet friends and keep at bay the world beyond our table. These domestic settings are ours and as locals rather than tourists, we can feel affronted when they are overrun by outsiders.

Not the same as home

In a tiny town south of Bologna we were the only guests in a converted paper mill. It snowed every day. Luca, our handsome host, built up the open fire in the sitting room each morning and left us with a pile of firewood. We read and ate and watched the outside world blur into whiteness, cocooned, safe and warm. It did *feel* a little like home. But our short stay, and our fleeting relationship with our host, meant that there could be no depth of connection. The place never really entered us, and we never imbued it with our personality. It stopped snowing, we packed our bags and waved Luca goodbye. And, more tellingly, we never returned and I doubt that Luca ever thought of us again.

Our friendships have time to develop and mature at home. This is not to deny that we don't meet wonderful people on our travels and form lasting friendships. Of course strangers who come into our sphere, with their different perspectives, do much to enrich our lives. But friendship doesn't evolve from travel experiences or destinations. Friendships grow from sharing ourselves and discovering common interest with others. That can happen anywhere, especially at home.

Create a personal backstage

True sanctuary doesn't rely on amassing *stuff*. This is the lesson we've learned from tidying expert Marie Kondo, that simplification can bring joy. We discard what means little to us and keep those things that speak to our heart.

Contentment doesn't come from opulence and perfection. The best home-havens are those we've created through slow, natural accretion over time, with items that we have chosen because they give us pleasure *for their own sake*. It matters not what anyone else might think of them. Our own aesthetic judgement is all that counts, how our possessions fit into our lives and convey what we find gratifying. What feels right for our home is as much about personal preference as our favourite music or hobby.

In her book *Pilgrimages* the photographer Annie Leibovitz photographed the homes of famous people – homes that depict contentment. In place of extravagance, they exude a confident self-expression and a clear understanding of what's most important. There are library shelves overflowing with books; an old teddy bear rescued from childhood; quirky keepsakes and treasures; musical instruments; evidence of hobbies; and collections of all sorts, from tapestries to fossils. The Arts and Crafts Movement guru William Morris once said, 'Have nothing in your house that you do not know to be useful, or believe to be beautiful'. Leibovitz shows that everyone fashions their own interpretation of his words.

Her photographs demonstrate how interior decoration can be an intensely personal expression of living. Everything in these homes of famous people reflected their chosen way of life. Armchairs were arranged in a circle so that people faced each other for conversation – a higher priority than the design of furniture or its stylish placement (or for watching television). Simple needs triumphed over endless consumerism. There was no striving to meet someone else's concept of ideal. In the very mismatched-ness, the whole was made perfect. And if things were a little down-at-heel, a little shabby and unkempt, what mattered was that the home provided an environment in which its inhabitants could live contented, authentic and meaningful lives.

Whoever coined the old adage, it's the journey not the destination that matters, had never experienced a 21st century long-haul flight.

Trains of thought

'The sole cause of man's unhappiness is that he does not know how to stay quietly in his room.'

Blaise Pascal

Armchair travelling

A seat on a plane can take us to distant lands, but so can an armchair at home. Comfort and peace instead of check-in queues, customs, unwieldy luggage, swollen ankles and utter tedium. Whoever coined the old adage, it's the journey not the destination that matters, had never experienced a 21st century long-haul flight.

At home in an armchair we can fly free and easy, listening to music and podcasts, reading books, watching films, or simply daydreaming. Flight without emissions. Indeed, the lowest of low-carbon pastimes.

We usually associate armchair travel with flicking through others' holiday photos on Instagram, reading travel books, studying google maps, exploring travel websites and reading blogs, or taking virtual tours. Or being transported to another place by reading Jack Kerouac's *On the Road*, or Peter Mayle's *A Year in Provence*.

But it can also mean letting our mind drift and meander where it will, to get lost in our thoughts, our head in the clouds. We can savour the chance to hear ourself think. We can look about and notice the details of our surroundings rather than confining our sights to what we need to see to meet a particular purpose.

Such whimsical ventures can lead us to serendipity – a wonderful word that comes from an ancient Persian folktale. The three princes of Serendip made an art of finding value in things not sought for, accidentally stumbling upon discoveries rather than actively seeking them through concerted effort.

It's an attractive notion – encountering the unexpected – yet we allow so little opportunity for serendipity to take hold. Something catches our eye but we've no time to linger. A new thought pops into our head, but there are so many pressing needs, we don't let it develop. No time to watch our children. No time to enjoy the sunset, or shifting cloud patterns, or the play of wind across water. No time to reflect on the plot of the book we're reading, or the dream we had last night.

In *A Room of One's Own*, Virginia Woolf sits on the bank of a river lost in thought.

Thought ... had let its line down into the stream. It swayed, minute after minute, hither and thither among the reflections and the weeds, letting the water lift it and sink it, until – you know the little tug – the sudden conglomeration of an idea at the end of one's line: and then the cautious hauling of it in, and the careful laying of it out?

A serendipitous thought, an idea, a memory, a vision – as delicate as thistledown. It will dissolve unrealised unless we stop and pay it the attention it deserves.

Take time to daydream

Busyness has come to define our lives. On one hand it signifies lots of wonderful things to do, on the other it highlights our fear of empty hours. We associate busyness with status and worry that others will judge our apparent time wasting and find us wanting. Even when we have the free time of holidays we are just as likely to cram the days with more busyness – such as itinerary-packed travel.

We often view travel as a chance for time out, to relax and daydream away from the pressures of home. But we don't really need a setting of drinks by a pool at a fancy foreign hotel to relax. Staycations make it so much easier to practise the indulgence of idleness. They can be a time when we reacquaint ourselves with the day's natural rhythms and instead of planning, let our thoughts lead us where they will. A time to recapture the simple art of daydreaming.

Find balance

The Italians have a delightful saying, dolce far niente – the sweetness of doing nothing. Far from laziness, dolce far niente is the art of knowing how to balance work and rest. Nonna spends the morning making tagliatelle exactly to the decreed measure (in Bologna, 6.5–7mm wide when raw, 8mm cooked – exactly). An afternoon's idleness – sitting in the doorway in the sunshine, watching the street – is her well-earned reward. These days, we might translate dolce far niente into me time, but this term robs the concept of its grace, hinting at selfishness instead of the *earned* luxury of repose.

Daydreaming improves memory and creativity, reduces stress and lowers blood pressure. It makes us better problem-solvers and better empathisers. It's through daydreaming that we come to clarify our thoughts, having the time and mental space to think an idea through, enjoying the internal journey of discovery.

We can gaze out the window, lie on the grass and watch the clouds, take a siesta. It's our break, our home, our choice. There's all the time in the world.

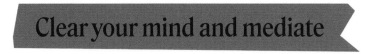

Clear your mind and mediate

We often think of travel as a means of reducing stress and increasing happiness. But there's a much easier path to improved wellbeing that doesn't require us to leave home.

With meditation we discover happiness and peace not through external stimuli but by reaching deep into ourselves. While there are any number of meditation retreats and tourism packages, usually at expensive, exotic locations, neither distance nor new surroundings nor expenditure are needed for meditation to bring significant change to our life. It can be practised anywhere and at any time. More importantly it is most beneficial when we introduce it as a routine part of our every day.

Staycations are the perfect opportunity to adopt meditation as a lifetime habit. We can create our own special oasis of calm and quiet at home to begin this journey into our inner mind, to cultivate stillness and find peace and happiness. Meditation is not difficult to master but it does require guidance, at least at first. Fortunately, there are any number of apps and YouTube videos offering instruction and there are sure to be classes available close to home.

If travel is an escape from home, meditation is an inner vacation. It is a genuine way of discovering ourselves. We attend to our inner selves, training our minds to focus on the present moment. By paying close attention to our bodies, thoughts and emotions we come to see and understand them more clearly. Meditation helps us to live more meaningful lives of contentment, compassion and curiosity.

Be mindful

By training our mind to stay in the present moment we encourage mindfulness. This state of being isn't confined to the time we spend meditating, it spills over to become an integral part of how we live. Constant alertness and self-awareness of our thoughts and feelings gives us greater control over our actions. We come to understand what causes stress and practise what relieves it. What brings happiness and what enhances it. We are kinder to ourselves and to others; less judgemental and more empathetic and accepting. We learn to appreciate what we have instead of craving more or taking life for granted.

We go a long way to answering the question: how should I live?

Relearn play, rediscover fun

Play comes in any number of forms, whatever brings us joy. It might be watching a movie or playing a board game. It can be creating and uploading a video, taking a role in the local theatre production, joining the kids on the jungle-gym, or tossing a stick for the dog. What all play has in common is that it's for the in-the-moment experience, not for the outcome. Play is not goal oriented; it's enjoyment for its own sake.

Play is something we adults feel we can't indulge in because we associate it with wasting time. This is a pity because there is plenty of evidence to show that play is as beneficial for us as it is for children. Regardless of age, play strengthens the mind, body and spirit. It brings surprise and delight. It wards off depression. It's as essential as sleep.

We make time to have fun with our partner to build and strengthen our relationship; with our children and grandchildren to relive the carefree joy of childhood; with our pets to share their unfettered exuberance. Play becomes an expression of our love.

It seems to come easier when we're away from home and work. It's as if the distance and anonymity release us from conformity and give us licence to let our hair down. However, for play to be truly beneficial, we can't wait for our annual holidays, we need to introduce it into our everyday lives. This is not to say we want to regularise play. It works best when it is spontaneous. How to be a little bit crazy and impulsive? The first step is to give ourselves permission. Relish the frivolity and fun.

Carpe diem – seize the moment for play whenever and wherever it arises.

Rainy day holidays

We have all experienced holidays where the weather has let us down. Rain, snow or even too much heat confine us indoors instead of heading out to explore. They force us to find new and creative ways of being entertained, they teach us to be self-motivated instead of relying on consuming readymade experiences. Many of these holidays, instead of being disappointments, become wonderful memories.

Why leave such creativity for rainy days away? There are so many ways to make indoor holidays at home fun and memorable.

Journey inside a book

Books. They should rank amongst the Seven Wonders of the World. Books shape our lives, they change us as surely as any journey. Older than travel, stories are humanity's most valuable and enduring tradition. They teach us what to value, who to trust, where to place our hope. Like daydreaming and play, reading a good book is never time wasted.

Unlike a play or a film, there is no intermediary when we read. Our interpretations are our own, reflecting what we know of life. That's why book club discussions can become so lively, as we debate the intentions of the writer, the behaviour of characters, the significance of the plot.

With a good book and an armchair, we can go anywhere without generating emissions or incurring expense. We transcend our surroundings to visit the houses of Bath in Jane Austen's *Persuasion*; surf the coast of Western Australia with Tim Winton in *Breath*; explore the streets of Ireland through Sally Rooney's *Normal People*.

There's no end to places we can go through the pages of books. Russia? Try Amor Towle's *A Gentleman in Moscow*. Norway? Sigrid Undset's *Kristin Lavransdatter*. Harare? *This Mournable Body* by Tsitsi Dangarembga. Madras? *Small Days and Nights* by Tishani Doshi.

Like globetrotting, there are books that cross continents, from fast-moving Dan Brown thrillers to Isabella Hammad's *The Parisian*, which travels from Montpellier and Paris to Palestine and the Middle East. Choose a destination, search the internet, visit a bookshop or library, get the book.

When we choose a book we are full of anticipation, ready for new discoveries. Opening a new book is like arriving at an airport, there is much to go through before we settle into the journey. In the early pages we must adjust to the writer's style, re-orient ourselves to a different place and time, get to know strangers. And then, when the book is good, we take off and our routine lives fall away behind us into the jet stream.

The book is the journey, the writer our guide, showing us the sights in the most sensory ways down to the most minute, intriguing details. And then further, deeper into places that we can never visit because they're inaccessible, or set in another time, or so fantastical as to be impossible to experience in real life. They open up the border between exterior and interior life for a more intense, richer, more meaningful understanding of universal human nature.

Books.
They should rank
amongst the
Seven Wonders
of the World.

A traveller's guide

Like most people, I love Venice. But I hate the crowds, the cruise ships that tower over and diminish the city, and the once quirky shops now given over to imported junk. For Venice's sake, we should stay away and let the locals be.

There are no crowds to stand between us and the pages of John Julius Norwich's remarkable *A History of Venice*. Between the covers we can smell the dank swamp of its Dark Age beginnings; witness the arrival of St Mark's kidnapped corpse; watch as the galleys are built in preparation for world trade domination. In our mind's eye, we can lose ourselves along the winding calles; punt the dark and mysterious canals; bear witness to the intrigues of the Doges; accompany prisoners across the Bridge of Sighs on their way to torture. Norwich captures all the intrigue and enchantment of Venice, from the minutest detail to San Marco's grandeur. Through this narrated journey we come to appreciate what makes Venice magical – an expansive illumination light years beyond what can be learned from a brief visit.

Different books reveal Venice from different angles. In the company of locally born Commissario Guido Brunetti, of Donna Leon's detective novels, we can become acquainted with the criminal elements of modern Venice. Thomas Mann's classic *Death in Venice* gives us yet another view of the city: a haunting place of obsession, contagion and death.

A cook's tour

'Not what we have but what we enjoy,
constitutes our abundance.'

Epicurus

Food adventures

How adventurous the ancient days of food trade must have been. How romantic those long, perilous expeditions now seem, with their discoveries of novel aromas and tastes to ignite the imagination and excite the senses. Grains and oranges, sugar and salt, olive oil and wine, coffee and tea, saffron and ginger.

Procuring food can still be an exciting, inspiring adventure knowing the reward will be a flavour-filled feast. The greatest risk these days is not finding a vacant parking spot near the market on a Saturday morning, but the discovery that figs are finally in season bestows a moment of sheer bliss.

The Tsukiji Fish Market in Tokyo, Pike Place Market in Seattle, La Merced in Mexico City and others attract hordes of tourists but their primary role remains unchanged. They still meet the culinary and nutritional needs of the local population. Big or small, city or rural, specialised or general, it is the grounded-ness of food markets that keeps them authentically distinctive and reflective of place.

There's nothing static about fresh-food markets. As places become more multicultural, as food trends change, so do markets. We're as likely to find peaked mountains of autumn-hue spices in Canada as in Morocco. The red chillies piled up in baskets at a Stockholm market will be taken home to unleash their heat in a Thai curry.

At home, we can
make time to go food
exploring and register
that the variety of food
on offer is as wide-ranging
as anywhere.

Share a recipe

There are so many ways to enjoy and share the pleasure of good food. Swapping recipes is one way, not unlike lending and borrowing books. We try a new dish and know instinctively who amongst our friends will appreciate this particular blend of ingredients. Or we beg for our next-door neighbour's orange cake recipe.

How old, I wonder, is this custom? Did those traversing the spice route swap recipes? How else would anyone have come to know how to use those mysterious new ingredients? A piece of *tree bark*? Cinn-a-mon you call it? What do you do with it?

The pleasure of new taste sensations never fades. Even today a Yotam Ottolenghi recipe can introduce us to new ingredients like rose harissa and pomegranate molasses. We search out the ingredients, try the dish, share it with friends, and exclaim over the new flavours.

At home, we can make time to go food exploring and register that the variety of food on offer is as wide-ranging as anywhere. On our travels, we might gaze at the glorious displays of food as a tourist attraction. At home, we shop with purpose. The transactions are a bona fide part of our daily lives.

Go fresh

Fresh-food markets feed all the senses. The textures of cheese, multicoloured vegetables and pyramids of glistening olives, the sea-tang smell of fish, the aroma of freshly baked bread. There are morsels of salami to sample. Buckets overflowing with flowers, each competing in fragrance and colour. Traders loudly yodelling their specials, shoppers propped up at counters sipping café lattes. Belle figura displays everywhere – that glorious Italian tradition dictating that carefully and beautifully curated presentation is as important as the items being displayed. There's an intensity to the place, a feeling that this is life at both its most elemental and – yes – sophisticated.

People from all walks of life, all backgrounds and ages come together with a common sense of purpose. The easy mixing is an essential part of the vibe. The shared activity, choosing and buying good food, creates an atmosphere that is both enlivening and harmonious. Relationships between traders and shoppers spring up and, over time, evolve into friendships, unforced and genuine. Third-generation customers buy from third-generation traders, appreciating their expertise, trusting their advice. These connections, initiated through food, are largely under-appreciated and yet so congenial when forged.

Bringing the farm to town

Who would have thought a few decades ago it would be possible to buy fresh seasonal produce amidst the congestion of New York City? To actually talk to the people who collected the eggs or harvested the corn, caught the fish or raised the sheep?

Union Square Farmers' Market – one of fifty farmers' markets in New York – does just that. It began in 1976 with just a few traders. These days, it hosts around 140 regional producers serving around 60,000 shoppers. It is possible to brush shoulders with the latest celebrity chef, Michelin-starred restauranteur or the women who run a soup kitchen downtown.

On the other side of the earth, in the village where I live (population 1000), our farmers' market takes place every second Saturday of the month. Metung is about as different from New York City as it's possible to imagine, with its small cluster of shops around the Village Green.

Like farmers' markets everywhere, ours is a local institution. We are warmed by the knowledge that we are amongst our own community. This is where we belong and who we belong with. It's a rare and precious feeling. An outsider might see something different, quaint might come to mind, as they watch we locals greet each other (traders, shoppers, even dogs) or as we munch on sausages in a blanket of bread cooked by a local charity. To us, it is simply the real thing, made purposeful because what we are buying is the very sustenance of life. We will take our purchases home and make soup for the family. Fill our house with the fragrance of flowers. Break fresh bread with friends.

At farmers' markets we relearn the value of provenance. The baker can tell us about where she sources her organic flour. The orchardist can tell us that the apples are free of chemical sprays and picked that morning. The farmer can explain that his cattle were pasture-raised. The cheesemaker can name her goats. Freshness, ripeness and taste – not appearance – are all-important. What's in season. No food miles. No nitrogen. No broccoli under plastic wrap for two weeks.

Farmers' markets embrace land health and animal welfare, community and education. We feel connected to the natural order of things, how food and its procurement should be.

A growing interest

Growing food is another pleasure. We can stand in the vegetable garden or hover over a row of pot plants and decide what's ready to harvest and what we'll cook for dinner. Letting our garden dictate what we will eat is the natural world putting us in our place. Is there anything more rewarding than sharing our garden's abundance with family, friends and neighbours?

Allotments and community gardens take root in places where backyards are rare but the desire to have hands in the soil is strong. These precious urban spaces, dedicated to growing food rather than buildings, are neighbourhood victories over developers. Outside the gates there might be a snarling urban jungle of concrete and congestion, but within there are lush plantings and whimsical artworks, chicken coups and compost bins. On a sunny Saturday morning, the gardeners gather to tend their plants, share seedlings and stories, pick the weekend's fare. Families picnic, someone might play a flute. In the way that good things overlap, community gardens, encompassing health, inclusion and learning, are up there with the best ways to spend our time.

Hunt and gather

Staycations give us time to experiment with food – shopping, cooking, sharing. Our search for ideas and ingredients can lead us to food shops we haven't visited before. At each place, we can ask for suggestions and advice, discuss the merits of one ingredient over another, and discover how others approach cooking and dining. We can experiment with something we haven't tried before – perhaps a bitter melon, dried mung beans or a cheaper cut of meat.

Grazing with the herd

There's more to eating than nourishment. As a way of bringing
people together, sharing food is a gesture as old as time. Companion,
a lovely word, derives from the Latin panis, meaning bread. It originally
described someone with whom we broke bread, that is, shared a meal.
We use food to give comfort and support. It mends feuds and banishes
loneliness; breaks down barriers and crosses borders. We use it to mark
life's milestones and to bring our family together. Whether it be picnics at
the beach, barbecues in the backyard or dinner parties in our home,
a shared meal with people we cherish is a way of celebrating life.

Most of us already embrace a variety of cuisines in our diets, clearly
illustrated by the range of restaurants in our midst. What a rewarding way to
learn more about foreign countries during our staycation. Rather than long
flight paths and layovers, we can map out a trip around our hometown that
takes in a multicultural mix of restaurants and food trucks. A taste excursion
with a new culinary destination every evening (for a fraction of the cost). While
big cities offer a cosmopolitan cornucopia of cuisine-specific eateries, a single
café in a small town is likely to feature a range of multicultural fare on its single
menu. In my tiny village, the baker sells Vietnamese pork rolls. The takeaway
sells Greek lamb souvlaki, Italian pizzas and very British fish and chips.

We don't have to dine out to become familiar with a broad range of cuisines.
We can try our hand at cross-cultural cooking at home. It seems every week,
a new cookbook is published, introducing us to cuisines from every corner
of the earth. Libraries, too, usually have an extensive range of cookbooks to
whet our appetite. It's so inspiring to open the pages of a cookbook to discover
obscure ingredients, time-saving techniques, unusual pairings of flavours
and inventive presentations. The rule is: there are no rules. Nothing stops
us from mixing the cuisine of one country with that of another. It's about
experimentation, imagination and enjoyment.

Our day might start with a Tunisian breakfast of shakshuka (eggs
poached in a spicy sauce); an Italian midday meal of taleggio cheese,
prosciutto, olives and ciabatta. And later, an evening feast of Peruvian aji
de gallina (creamy chicken casserole) served with boiled eggs, potatoes and
rice, with a Torrontés wine, followed by suspiro a la limeña (sticky caramel
topped with meringue). At this stage, we might need to go flâneuring.

Even if it wasn't possible to also fit in a Danish pastry for morning tea and baklava in the afternoon, we've toured three countries in one day. Do this for a week, and we'll be up to twenty-one countries – with 171 still to explore. We might not like everything we taste but at least we've had a try.

Researching menu ideas is fun. The choices are as wide as our imagination, and we can share our results with the people we love. Replete and happy amongst the remains of a sumptuous meal, we talk into the night about food and culture, and how the spirit of travel can be relished at home.

Shakshuka

I used to know shakshuka prosaically as 'Sunday Night Eggs', a quick and easy meal to end the weekend, served with a warmed baguette and glass of red wine. Then I discovered the Levanter Café in Melbourne. The shakshuka I ordered for breakfast was served with cardamom-spiced Turkish coffee. Morning or evening, it's a wholesome, tasty dish. Here's the recipe (for six people):

1 tbs olive oil
1 medium brown onion, diced
1 red capsicum (bell pepper), seeded and diced
3 cloves garlic, crushed
2 tsp paprika
1 tsp chilli power
400g canned diced tomatoes
salt, pepper
6 large free-range eggs
A handful each of fresh parsley and coriander (cilantro), chopped

Heat the oil in a pan and fry the onion and capsicum (pepper) until the onion is translucent – about 5 minutes. Add the garlic, paprika and chilli powder and cook for a further 3 minutes. Add the tomatoes and season with salt and pepper. Simmer the sauce for about 8 minutes. Using the back of a wooden spoon, make six hollows in the sauce and break an egg into each. Cover the pan and cook for a further 8 minutes, until the eggs have set. Garnish with parsley and coriander (cilantro). Serve hot - with Turkish coffee in the morning, shiraz at night.

Chart a new course

'The correct analogy for the mind is not a vessel that needs filling, but wood that needs igniting'.

Plutarch

Keep learning

Travel can be thought-provoking and educational. A stroll around the Arc de Triomphe helps us to understand the history of the Hotel National des Invalides, which informs our visit to La Madeleine, the Vendome Column and La Chateau de Malmaison. In Paris, Napoleon's legacy is everywhere, and our enjoyment of the city is enhanced by the slow accumulation of knowledge we gather from one famous site after another. We find ourselves asking questions, appraising, keen to know more. Our awakened interest can take us almost anywhere – into history, architecture, understanding the Napoleonic Code, researching the Empress Joséphine's art collections or learning to cook chicken marengo (reputedly Napoleon's favourite dish).

Learning takes effort. After all, a trip to Paris could be about nothing more than croissants and café au lait before heading to shop at Galeries Lafayette. But such activities don't stir our interest in the world; they don't stimulate inquisitiveness.

Unfortunately, despite our best intentions, the resolutions we make while holidaying – to learn more about what sparked our interest – soon disappear in the whirlwind of everyday. We abandon our plans to swot up on Napoleon's impact on 18th century Europe or to take a breadmaking course so that we can bake baguettes at home. When our plane touches down we fold our wings away, life takes over and we forget to fly into that wider world of knowledge.

Challenge yourself

If travel is moving *about*, learning is moving *forward*, orienting us in the direction of our future and setting us on a path towards a more rounded life. Lifetime learning is the continuous quest to add to our knowledge about anything and everything that interests us.

Travel-motivation websites routinely hijack Helen Keller's saying about life being either a daring adventure or nothing. But Keller was an educator, and there's nothing in her words to suggest we have to leave home to find adventure. Striving to learn is daring to be different – different from those who think there's no value in learning, different from our current self. It is an adventure all of its own, and learning at home can be every bit as exciting as climbing into an aeroplane.

Napoleon said, 'Until you spread your wings, you have no idea how far you can fly'. Unacquainted with Airbuses and Club Meds, he was thinking in terms of rising to the challenges we set ourselves.

It is a dare which, if taken, comes with a whole raft of enduring personal rewards and goes a long way towards finding meaning in life.

Ignite the spark

A staycation gives us the free time to embark on an interest divorced from the demands of work. Rather than improve our mastery of Excel, we can try our hand at poetry or welding; golf or mountaineering; ballroom dancing, yodelling or playing the harp. Our enjoyment of anything is heightened by greater knowledge.

Learning is only for kids? You can't teach old dogs new tricks? Science has debunked such catchphrases. It has also proved Aristotle wrong. The ancient philosopher likened memory to wax tablets – hot and pliable at birth, but gradually cooling and toughening with age. Recent research in neuroscience and psychology reveals that regardless of age, our brains retain their plasticity for absorbing new knowledge and the more we learn, the younger our brains become. While children have an advantage in some areas, we adult learners benefit from our experience and our capacity for analysis, self-reflection and discipline.

Do no harm

The citizens of Barcelona were reduced to putting up signs asking, if it's tourist season, does that mean we can shoot them? It was a cry of exasperation at the floods of tourists invading their city and their lives.

Learning does not impinge on anyone else's rights. It doesn't overwhelm communities, distort real estate values, or commodify traditions. Nor does it necessarily involve carbon footprints or footprints across fragile environments. Yet it still allows us to explore so many aspects of otherness, often in more depth than if we travelled. It is a journey largely within the mind, in pursuit of personal growth and development.

There doesn't need to be a monetary cost to learning at home. So much is available at little or no charge, from conversations with friends, to public lectures, to library resources, to internet offerings, to interpretive signage in public places. In these and other ways, learning is exceptionally varied, accessible and egalitarian.

The world at a click

When the pandemic confined us to home with time on our hands, something amazing happened. We discovered – or rediscovered – the satisfaction of learning something new. And because we were restricted to home, we enthusiastically embraced online learning and discovered how effortlessly it took us out into the world of fascinating facts and skills.

Every conceivable subject was searched and downloaded. We learnt to play a musical instrument, explored our family tree and created GIFs. With a click of YouTube, we learnt how to meditate and lift weights. We joined online yoga, tai chi and pilates workouts. Ballet schools offered free virtual classes. Even beginners had the opportunity to become adept at jeté, plié and pirouette.

We downloaded Duolingo and other apps to learn a new language. We followed instructions to build a chicken coop and become adept home-educators.

We took our sourdough baking to a whole new level (or not!).

We undertook research, accessing academic papers and library archives. We started college courses, and downloaded podcast.

We discovered that learning brings the world, in all of its amazing breadth and possibilities, home to us.

Culture online

A core value of our cultural organisations – both public and private – is to share their knowledge and stimulate learning. Having to close their doors during COVID-19 lockdowns, they took their charter to new heights, reaching out to us through technology instead of relying on us travelling to them.

They delivered exhibitions, plays, comedy, and music of every genre into our homes. And not only organisations. Individual artists everywhere turned their creative minds to the task of developing new ways for all of us to access the arts – ways that were innovative, fun and educative.

The J Paul Getty Museum invited us to re-create famous works of art using household objects. Some of the creations were outrageously funny and clever. The challenge led us to analyse the masterpieces, to study their compositions and use of colour so that we might replicate them. We couldn't help but learn while being amused.

Learn with others

Joining a class puts us in the presence of others, be it flower arranging or acting, dog grooming or an introduction to quantum physics. There are any number of studies that show that learning with others brings rewards beyond acquiring new knowledge. Whether this is physically in the same room or collectively online, a special rapport develops between those who share a learning experience. Each person brings with them the richness and diversity of their own life: their past experiences, their ideas and dreams, the ways in which they reason and problem solve. Our minds are nourished as much by each other as by the instructor and topic.

When we share a learning experience, we develop the skills of listening, questioning and debating. There is a world of difference between a thought rattling around in our heads and airing our views intelligibly in company. To share them, our propositions need to be considered and defendable. Examining and testing their soundness makes them more logical. The to-and-fro of debate requires us to pay attention to what others have to say. Even when we don't agree, listening to opposing opinions strengthens our own arguments and sharpens our critical thinking.

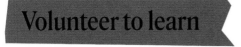

Volunteer to learn

Combining learning with volunteering is a true win-win situation. We extend a helping hand to those in need, *and* learn the particular skills required to fulfill the mission of the organisation we've joined.

There are options to suit all interests. Volunteering is not limited to meals-on-wheels and knitting knee rugs. Festival organisers are always looking for volunteers. We can indulge our passion for literature, comedy, music, food, dance – whatever – by giving our time. In return we'll gain insights that would otherwise forever elude us.

We can volunteer abroad and do tremendous good, but we can also volunteer from home for overseas missions. We can work alongside like-minded people, or we can contribute from our desk with a screen and keyboard.

Unsurprisingly, altruism is good for us personally. It also underpins community wellbeing and fosters a strong, caring, inclusive society.

Hobbies for happiness

Almost by definition, a hobby is something we have chosen to do because we find it interesting and stimulating. For many, travel is a hobby, although we make the most of travel when we do it *in pursuit* of a hobby – wildlife photography, steam trains, cooking, garden design and even Wagnerian opera. If we rely solely on travel, our hobby is limited to the times we spend away, whereas hobbies are best when we can pick them up any time we choose.

Having a hobby gives us something to look forward to. It takes our mind off problems, distracts us from boredom and overcomes fatigue. It makes our conversations more interesting. It sparks our creativity and rewards us with a sense of achievement. We focus on the indoor plants we're propagating or the wooden toy we're making or the jigsaw we're completing and our worries evaporate. When we see the plant flourishing, the kids having fun with the toy, the jigsaw puzzle completed, we experience a particular sort of thrill and a very personal *I did this* boost to our morale.

Anything learned contributes to the sum of who we are. It doesn't have to be grand to have merit. Far from trifling, hobbies are one good measure of living well. Like daydreaming and playing, we might dismiss hobbies as a waste of time, but that depends on what we are trying to achieve and how else we might use (or waste) that time. If we are looking for life balance and contentment, and if we admit that so much of our time is spent doing things that add no meaning to our lives, then hobbies – avenues for our creative urges, pathways to new friendships – start to look pretty good.

Hobbies can be pleasurable while also lightening our impact on the planet. Sewing for example. It doesn't have to be haute couture. A tote bag makes a good project or net bags for fruit and vegetable shopping or a mask. Homemade items that replace throw-away alternatives.

My sewing friend made a complete wardrobe of outfits during self-isolation, knowing that she had nowhere to wear her new creations. We decided that didn't matter. The reward was in the *doing*, not the *having*. In the moment of creation, nothing else exists. Sewing – any hobby – becomes a means of holding the world at bay. It becomes an act healing.

Ikigai

We travel to be stimulated by new sights and ideas, to meet new people, to shift gears in our lives. Learning does all of this, in flexible, enduring ways.

We travel to learn history and geography, a new language, self-confidence. At home, we can turn our mind to any topic for learning – at a fraction of the cost.

We travel to be challenged, to see how far we are prepared to venture into the unknown. But this is a limited and sometimes dubious quest. With lifelong learning, we set a goal and stretch ourselves until it is met. We add the outcome to our growing bank of knowledge. Then we repeat. Anywhere, at any time.

Learning is a positive journey through life, without a final destination but with inspirational stopovers all along the way. As the Japanese say, it fosters ikigai – finding meaning in life by realising hopes and dreams.

As the Japanese say, it fosters ikigai – finding meaning in life by realising hopes and dreams.

Check in with children

'Our war on nature must end.'

Greta Thunberg

What matters most

The best way for children to discover who they are is within the context of home, family, community and culture. They thrive in the place where they belong, amongst the people, customs and things that make up their everyday life. We know this from reams of research. Attachment, trust, security and routine matter most in children's lives.

So why do we subject them to crowds and queues at airports? The tedium and confinement of flights? The stress of being separated from home and friends? Sightseeing designed for adults with restrictions on their freedom to run and play?

The activities and ideas in this book are not poor substitutes for travel. They are alternatives that bestow enormous value and meaning in their own right. As a preparation for adult life and means of engendering self-respect, they are of far greater benefit than sightseeing. All of them can be introduced into children's lives with ease, bequeathing the best possible inheritance.

Music, art, books, sport, community engagement, immersion in nature. There are so many local, positive ways to keep a wide age-range keen and curious. Children develop affectionate ownership of the special places within their home orbit. This is *my* park, *my* library, *my* street, *my* museum. With repeated visits, they feel at ease and connected.

Museums cater for budding palaeontologists and aspiring botanists. Art galleries inspire creativity and free-thinking and often have child-centred narrations of the collections. Libraries lead the way into fantastic worlds through storytime activities that blend reading, singing, play and craft. A sensitive bookseller will suggest the perfect young adult novel. Orchestras perform concerts especially for the young (*Peter and the Wolf*, *The Carnival of the Animals* and movie themes like *Star Wars*). Magic and enchantment are at play in *The Nutcracker* and other ballets. Theatre opens a further door into the world of make-believe for the young and helps to untangle some of life's mysteries for teenagers.

Your local streets offer a whole host of secret places, mysteries and stories. I-spy turns walking into a game. Cafés serving different cuisines or festivals celebrating different cultural communities can broaden a child's world view as surely as a visit to a foreign land. At farmers' markets, children can discover the whole sensory gambit of fresh, unpackaged food. They can witness how buying food can be a lively, joyous, social occasion. They learn about good nutrition, seasonality and food miles. Here are the wellsprings of a child's developing sense of identity and belonging.

Nature and play

A child's world is sensory, more wondrous and multifaceted than our adult (or travel industry) imagination can conceive. They have their own interests, their own ideas about what is enjoyable. For them, there's more amazement in a rainbow, or a stick insect, or a clutch of blue eggs in a bird's nest than another marble statue or old building.

So little is needed to spark their imagination. A safe place that allows for uninterrupted, unstructured, self-directed, open-ended play. Time to let their mind wander, the opportunity to build their own imaginary worlds unmitigated through adult values and interests. A day of *doing* – making, cooking, gardening, building – is more fun and fulfilling than gaping at the world's top tourist sights. Planted at home, these lessons will sprout and blossom into a love of lifetime learning.

In his book, *Last Child in the Woods*, Richard Louv proposes the term nature-deficit disorder. He laments the way in which children are being insulated from nature and he sounds alarm bells of what happens to them, mentally and physically, when they don't spend time outdoors. He notes that our shift indoors, away from the natural world is startling, after millennia of human interaction and interdependence with nature.

Louv is just one commentator amongst many to assure us that children don't need big adventures or grand overseas vacations. Much more important is our guidance to help them awaken all their senses through interaction with their local natural environment.

The lure of the screen

Rebecca Solnit wrote of her childhood spent roaming outdoors, developing self-reliance, imagination, a desire to explore, a sense of direction and a taste for adventure. She compared her experience with today's children and wondered what will result from them being placed under house arrest. She wasn't referring to mandated self-isolation during COVID-19, but to the freely chosen path of staying indoors, staring at devices.

We adults have also erected screens between ourselves and the wider world. We are in the park playing with the kids and for a moment it's fabulously chaotic and full of laughter. We pull out our phone to take a photo and – oh no – we have a dozen alerts that must be read. Now. The magic disappears.

The outside world, with its everyday miracles, is a fascinating classroom where anything and everything offers a potential lesson. Sunrise and sunset; the changing shapes of clouds and the flight of birds. Storms, thunder and lightning, surf, rockpools, puddles. The first green shoots from a seed, the thrum of cicadas on a hot afternoon, the intricacy of a flower, the busyness of bees.

Adults easily forget to look. What a gift, then, to be reminded by children to observe. By spending time with them we get to see the world afresh through their young, eager eyes. They can keep us alert to the magic and mystery all around us.

An overflow of opportunities

Skateparks, waterparks, fun parks, farm parks. Playgrounds with merry-go-rounds and jungle gyms, sandboxes and seesaws. Mazes and treetop walks, flying foxes and swimming pools. These places of fun and games are recognised as being amongst the most important environments for children after their home. They encourage spontaneity, creative play, fitness, agility and social skills. They present challenges and cultivate curiosity and problem-solving.

Child's play

Children's gardens created within botanic gardens are designed for hiding, running, jumping, yelling, climbing trees, getting lost in mazes, weaving through forests, and getting drenched in fountains. All within an enclosed area that lets parents relax.

Full of sensory wonder, these gardens spark an interest in nature to help children to recognise their intimate connection – their biophilia. The children perceive that this magical natural world is worthy of respect and protection.

There's more to local parks than just playground equipment. There's mud for pies, sand for castles, dirt and sticks for drawing, stones for sculpture. Nature is great at providing all the tools to stimulate play and inspire imagination.

We could travel halfway around the globe to camp in a world-famous national park or we could help the kids to pitch a tent in a local camping ground or even the backyard. Do children really care about the name and fame of a place, even if it does feature in all the travel brochures? What's important is the adventure of sleeping outdoors under canvas; toasting marshmallows over a campfire; catching a fish on a line or an owl in a torch beam; going without a bath.

For children, holidays are like exclamation marks – punctuated interludes that forge lasting memories. Simplicity answers for this at least as well as lavishness. A week spent camping near home, mucking about with other camping kids, can be every bit as wonderful and memorable, and as packed with fun and surprise as a budget-stretching, stress-inducing trip to Disneyland. And just think what else we can do for our children with the money we've saved. Tickets to events, a new bike, a guitar, surfing lessons, books or a night out at a new café. Rather than one spree, exclamation marks can be spread throughout the year.

Pockets of holiday

Staycations give us the time to experiment with play, to discover what our kids love most. We can set them in motion and let them find their means of fun, absorption and creativity in their own way. They can learn to turn boredom into initiative and self-motivation. While they're entertaining themselves, we can enjoy watching. Simple, rewarding, therapeutic, repeatable occasions.

Rather than abandoning this discovery when we return to our everyday routine, we can slot times for play into our busy lives as holiday pockets. We can schedule these pockets as we would any other appointment to give them the priority they deserve. We learn to accept the idea that having nothing serious to do in an otherwise hectic day is okay. It's more than okay–it's terrific. And it's great for the kids.

Holidays for the future

The internet is awash with encouragements to take children travelling. Terms such as world-schooling and edventuring are used to convince us that it's *unquestionably* a good thing. Travel does have a place in igniting a child's curiosity and wonder, stimulating imagination and teaching adaptability, building self-confidence and instilling tolerance. However, it takes only a touch of inspiration and a little planning to create a staycation that achieves all of these advantages, while avoiding negatives such as the expense, stress and environmental impact.

By reducing our travel carbon footprints, we are taking steps towards ensuring that our children will inherit a planet that remains habitable.

If children expect to travel overseas like their friends it's up to us to explain the benefits of staying home. It's not as if they aren't already aware of the climate crisis. We've seen how children, in many places, are leading the charge in demanding change because they know what's at risk. The student strike movement FridaysForFuture has spread across the globe. The United Nations is giving a youth advisory group their say on climate action.

Count the cost

If that big holiday is going to strain the family budget to breaking point, increase tension and put constraints on what can be done for the remainder of the year, why do it? Well, yes, it would be amazing for the kids to see lions roaming about a wildlife sanctuary in Africa. But as with questioning our own reasons for travel, what, in essence and in truth, do we want children to gain from such an experience?

For a tiny fraction of the cost of taking the family to Africa, a visit to a zoo in our city (one that practises professional standards of animal care) will do all that is needed to ignite children's curiosity and wonder. Within a safe environment, children can explore and discover animals from the arctic, insects from the Amazon and their own native fauna. The planet's stunning diversity of lifeforms is laid before them and they can begin to appreciate their own place in nature's order. What they don't get to see the first time round, they can see next time.

More than an exhibition of captive animals, the best zoos these days are conservation organisations, making serious contributions to protecting threatened species through practice, advocacy and research. They co-operate with like-minded institutions from around the world to study the earth's varied habitats and to manage projects that will sustain communities and wildlife.

These zoos understand their role in children's lives, too. They offer a wide range of activities – from informative to thrilling – to engender a sense of wonder in and care for the natural world. A trip to the zoo might not be as exotic as a wildlife safari, but it ticks a lot of boxes for parents, children, the household budget, the animal world, and the planet.

We've seen how children, in many places, are leading the charge in demanding change because they know what's at risk.

A journey for life

Resilience, adaptability and self-knowledge are the skills today's children will need to carry them into an unpredictable future. Most of the information they learn today will be of scant use to them in a few decades' time. The key survival tools will be self-awareness, inner strength and personal agency. These qualities will be their means of coping with the stresses that change inflicts. Self-confidence will determine whether one controls one's life or is controlled by someone or something else.

The most purposeful travel we can undertake with children will be journeying with them into the mysteries of life, instilling curiosity and wonder. If we guide them towards a greater capacity for contemplation and reflection while introducing them to all the colour, depth and intrinsic value of cultural pursuits, we will lay strong foundations for their future success.

If we want a habitable planet for today's children and for all future generations, we need to change our ways to reduce greenhouse gases. It's simply a matter of re-prioritising and deciding what is most important. It's a matter of thinking independently rather than following the herd; of knowing we don't have to spend heaps and consume heaps to achieve happiness. Our key question *How should I live?* includes *How should I live in a way that is best for my children – now and into the future?*

Afterword

This place in time

'Act as if what you do makes a difference. It does.'

William James

Virtue from necessity

In the 18th century, Welsh miners were too poor to buy musical instruments but they could use their voices for free. And so they formed choirs. With voices raised, they sang of their country, their struggles, their faith.

These days, Welsh Male Voice Choirs are treasured both in Wales and throughout the world. Their homeland has become known as the Land of Song and their voices contribute to the preservation of their distinctive language and traditions.

Can we be like the instrument-lacking Welsh and find an alternative to travel, not only because circumstances – climate change, pandemic – require it of us, but as a choice that grows into something significant in its own right? Can we make a virtue out of the new necessities that now confront us?

The spirit of travel does not rely solely on going far away. We can stay local and still be transported by theatre, art, a beautiful garden or a good book. There's wonder to be found in a perfect musical phrase and a ravishing sunrise. Curiosity at home can send us out onto the streets, to get to know our neighbourhood and our neighbours. We can expand our horizons by taking up a hobby or joining a club. We can get to know people from other lands – in a street close by, or a café down the road. We can come to know more about the world by visiting a library or museum.

With a shift of focus we can fashion our staycations so that they are every bit as intriguing and rewarding as travel. With planning and practice, we can become as accomplished at home holidays as the Welsh became at singing.

With a little imagination and planning, our staycations can satisfy most of those promises and needs locally, less expensively, and more effortlessly repeatable.

Change for the better

In a 1928 essay, D.H. Lawrence wrote:

Superficially, the world has become small and known. Poor little globe of earth, the tourists trot round you as easily as they trot round the Bois or round Central Park. There is no mystery left, we've been there, we've seen it, we know all about it. We've done the globe and the globe is done.

It has taken us nearly 100 years to catch up to Lawrence. And in that time, our poor little globe of earth has been ravaged almost beyond recognition. Travel, of course, is not solely to blame. And there will always be travel, wanderlust and other reasons will continue to draw us away. But whether we like it or not, our decisions regarding travel are now laced with a moral imperative. The earth and future generations urgently need us to change our ways. Computer-generated journeys and virtual-reality tourism will have their place, curing some travel-bug pangs without adding emissions, but they can offer little more than entertainment and distraction.

And what of all those travel promises? And all the reasons why we think we must travel? With a little imagination and planning, our staycations can satisfy most of those promises and needs locally, less expensively, and more effortlessly repeatable. We don't ask or expect too much of our time at home, and in this frame of mind, our expectations are forever exceeded. All the good things we discover and learn can readily be incorporated into our everyday lives as potent, enduring wonders. How those Welsh miners must have felt when they lifted their voices and realised that they didn't need accompaniment to make beautiful music.

If we are to have any control over the future, we will need to look for earnest and substantive answers to what it means to live a good, purposeful life. The answers, surely, will be found within our culture and community, in the way they carve out for us a personal place in the world and give us strength, hope and inspiration.

Here, at home, with all that it has to offer, we can begin to map out a way to achieve meaning in life. If we are alert, the world will come to us.

About the author

Travel and tourism have long been a part of Jenny Herbert's life; she has worked in the tourism industry for more than 20 years, is a keen traveller and author of the best-selling *The Intelligent Traveller: how to plan your perfect trip.*

The world turns and this book – *The Art of Being a Tourist at Home* – is born from a growing concern about how our travelling ways have impacted on communities and the environment, and a recognition of how easily we can indulge the spirit of travel close to home.

Jenny is the author of *The Intelligent Traveller: how to plan your perfect trip* and *In the Shadow of a Hero*. She lives in regional Victoria, Australia with her husband Fred.

With thanks

Many people, from many institutions, gave me invaluable insights:
John Nolan, Melbourne Symphony Orchestra
Rebekah Marks, State Library of Victoria
Chris Mead, Melbourne Theatre Company
Kerry Walker, actor
Caterina Palman, Melbourne Visitor Hub, City of Melbourne
Carolyn Meehan, Melbourne Museum
Shauna Jones, Parks Victoria
Jaclyn Crupi, Hill of Content bookshop
Clare McAlister, architect
Robin Penty, Royal Botanic Gardens Victoria
Rohini Kappadath, Immigration Museum, Melbourne
Anjali Nambissan, Ethnic Culture Commission
Victor Chan and Bettina DeChateaubourg, Queen Victoria Market
Lydia Griffiths and Nathan Lange, Creativity Australia With One Voice choir
Katie Russell, National Gallery of Australia
Nancy Langham-Hooper, art historian
Elena Brooks, Asylum Seeker Resource Centre
Angela Hudson, about learning
Justine Adams, about children
Special thanks to my early readers:
Rob Trenberth
Anna Cook
Rob Cook
Helmy Cook
Geoffrey Conaghan
Mathew Erbs
Liz Clay
Janie Cohen
Sara Rose
Andy Phalp
Jenny Dalgleish
Thanks to Di Johnston for her ongoing enthusiasm and encouragement. And to the people who took my manuscript and created something much better: editor Amanda McMahon, and Hardie Grant's senior editor Megan Cuthbert, publisher Melissa Kayser and designer Ngaio Parr.
And to Fred, for so much willing help with this book and for everything else.

Published in 2021 by Hardie Grant Travel,
a division of Hardie Grant Publishing

Hardie Grant Travel (Melbourne)
Building 1, 658 Church Street
Richmond, Victoria 3121

Hardie Grant Travel (Sydney)
Level 7, 45 Jones Street
Ultimo, NSW 2007

www.hardiegrant.com/au/travel

All rights reserved. No part of this
publication may be reproduced, stored in
a retrieval system or transmitted in any
form by any means, electronic, mechanical,
photocopying, recording or otherwise,
without the prior written permission of
the publishers and copyright holders.

The moral rights of the author have
been asserted.

Copyright text © Jenny Herbert 2021
Copyright concept and design © Hardie
Grant Publishing 2021

A catalogue record for this
book is available from the
National Library of Australia

Hardie Grant acknowledges the
Traditional Owners of the country on
which we work, the Wurundjeri people of
the Kulin nation and the Gadigal people
of the Eora nation, and recognises their
continuing connection to the land, waters
and culture. We pay our respects to their
Elders past, present and emerging.

The Art of Being a Tourist at Home
ISBN 9781741177107

10 9 8 7 6 5 4 3 2 1

Publisher Melissa Kayser
Project editor Megan Cuthbert
Editor Amanda McMahon
Proofreader Lesley Bruynesteyn
Design Ngaio Parr
Typesetting Hannah Schubert

Colour reproduction by
Splitting Image Colour Studio

Printed and bound in China by
LEO Paper Products LTD.

FSC
www.fsc.org
MIX
Paper from
responsible sources
FSC® C020056

The paper this book is printed on is
certified against the Forest Stewardship
Council® Standards and other sources.
FSC® promotes environmentally
responsible, socially beneficial and
economically viable management of
the world's forests.